How to Write Creative Non-fiction

Donna Kay Kakonge

Donna Kakonge

How to Write Creative Non-fiction

Donna Kay Kakonge, M.A. – Sole Proprietor dkakonge@sympatico.ca
dkakonge@gmail.com
http://kakonged.wordpress.com
www.donnakakonge.com

Core Competencies:
Education
Journalism
Broadcast Writing
Book Publishing
Visual Arts
Law

Since 1992, Donna Kakonge has freelanced in the cultural and performing arts, as well as worked in the government sector. She began by working on a breakthrough show for youth called "Road Movies" which aired on CBC. Following this, she worked at the local, national and international levels of both CBC Radio and Television, mainly in Toronto. Kakonge was involved with the start of a first-ever morning show aired on shortwave to sub-Saharan Africa called "African Eyes." While an Announcer/ Producer for this show, she was sent on special assignment to Edmonton to meet Canadian diplomats and Nigerian author/activist Dr. Wole Soyinka.

Kakonge has also worked for the Discovery Channel, Discovery Channel International, Vision-TV (for now S-Vox), and the BBC. She keeps up with the latest technology in broadcasting by maintaining a podcast online and has produced a CD of radio documentaries, as well as two audio downloads narrated by her that are available on Lulu.com.

She has done television appearances as a spokesperson for the Ministry of Health and Long-Term Care's Tele-Health program through commercials that aired all over Ontario, as well as guest appearances on the W Network, Food Network and "Breakfast Television." She has been a fashion model for print and runway, represented by Tony Eastwood Talent Agency which also represented Neve Campbell at the same time. She has done art modeling for the Toronto Art School, Etobicoke School of the Arts, Durham College, Arts and Letters Club, Maxx the Mutt Animation School and many others. Currently she is the show host and producer of "Ideal Job" with Donna Magazine.

Art modeling was not Kakonge's first time in the classroom. She assisted in teaching undergraduate and graduate students at Carleton University in Ottawa. She also received a Bachelor of Journalism degree from this school and received an award funded by now Senator Pamela Wallin. She assisted and also had sole-responsibility for classes taught at Makerere University in Kampala, Uganda, as well as closer to home at Concordia University in Montréal. She speaks French fluently.

She has taught journalism at the University of Guelph-Humber and Humber College. She has taught Canadian Broadcasting and Online Marketing at Trebas Institute, as well as Skills for College English at George Brown College. Kakonge has also taught ESL at Sullivan Language Learning Centre in Montréal, Institute Provincial in Montréal and TEC Inc. Other teaching experiences include the day programs in Seneca College's and Centennial College's journalism programs. With Seneca she taught York University students in the joint program and with Centennial, University of Toronto students in the joint program. She has also taught Dramatic Writing at Ryerson University's Chang School of Continuing Education. Recently she taught Magazine Journalism and Journalism Career Management with Centennial College. Both courses were taught online.

Kakonge is a PhD Candidate at OISE/University of Toronto in Curriculum, Teaching and Learning Development. Kakonge is working on her dissertation focusing on the career aspirations of black female high school students in Toronto. She is also doing a law degree online with the University of London International Programmes. She recently received a TESOL certificate from LinguaEdge and has a Master of Arts degree in Media Studies from Concordia University where she built a website back in 1999 called Salon Utopia that included her own artwork, photographs and creative stories. She has also taken numerous courses in languages, creative writing, script-writing and broadcasting. She recently received a Québecor Documentary Fellowship that ended in 2009. She has presented at many conferences and worked for the provincial government in the Ministry of Citizenship and Immigration. She worked as an Assistant Editor on the Journal of Curriculum and Pedagogy and a Teaching Assistant with the University of Toronto Mississauga campus. She works as a Facilitator with Hetta Institute (coming up again soon), and worked as an Online English Teacher with Weblish Pal and Tutor Doctor. She currently takes private clients for writing and English coaching. She also offers life coaching and services to help people write their memoir and biography books. She also worked as a Writer with the University of Toronto. In the fall of 2011 she taught five sections of Global Citizenship with Centennial College. She works as a Teacher Education Program Assistant at OISE/University of Toronto, Associate Faculty/ Course Developer with Yorkville University, an Educational Assistive Technology Expert with The Study School and as Adjunct Faculty with Florida University of Health and Sciences.

Kakonge is the author or contributor to 44 books that are mainly self-published and published by Lulu.com (http://stores.lulu.com/kakonge). One is published by Concordia University called Headlight Anthology. The Totally Unknown Writers Festival Collection 2011 is her latest published contribution (http://www.liferattle.ca/ publishing/2011festivalstories.html). She has an upcoming narrative non-fiction book titled How to Talk to Crazy People which is self-published. She is also working on a new book titled Three Quarters, also to be self-published for September 2013. Since
2007, she has had a multimedia online magazine called Donna (http://kakonged.wordpress.com) which is currently top-ranked in Google. She has academic publications published and in process of publication with the International Conference in New Horizons in Education 2012 (where she is also a virtual presenter), The International Global Education Conference 2012 (where she is also a virtual presenter), Global Citizen Digest with Centennial College and a completed publication with Media, Mind, Society with OISE to name a few. Kakonge has also published a number of journalistic work with New Dreamhomes and Condominiums Magazine, one editorial in the Toronto Star and a number of stories with Pride Newsmagazine for African-Canadians. She has presented or will be presenting at 34 conferences and has received approximately 40 awards in her adult livelihood. Kakonge will have her dissertation Young Black Women in Toronto High Schools: Portraits of Family,

School and Community Involvement in Developing Goals and Aspirations published through Nsemia Inc. Publishers in 2014. Crazy People Talking Sane will be available on Lulu.com in 2015.

BOOKS AND CDS BY DONNA KAKONGE

Totally Unknown Writers Festival Collection 2011

How To Talk To Crazy People: Vignettes of Sixteen Breakdowns

Young Black Women in Toronto High Schools: Portraits of Family, School and Com- munity Involvement in Developing Goals and Aspirations (upcoming)

For more please visit: www.donnakakonge.com

FIRST EDITION LULU INTERNATIONAL EDITION, December 2008

Copyright 2013 by Donna Kay Kakonge, M.A.

All rights researched under International and Pan-American Copyright Conventions. Published in the United States by Lulu.com.

National Archives of Canada Cataloguing in Publication Data

Kakonge, Donna
How to Write Creative Non-fiction
ISBN: 978-0-9810797-1-4

Book Design by Dreamstime.com

Manufactured in the United States.

To Oshun and Talise

HOW TO WRITE CREATIVE NON-FICTION

INTRODUCTION

Through the power of the Internet, the popularity of www.donnakakonge.com and Donna Magazine: http://kakonged.wordpress.com the knowledge of the writer – me, Donna Kakonge – I bring to you effective tools and tips for writing creative non-fiction.

This ebook is meant to prepare you for the world of creative non-fiction writing and to make a living at it either full-time, part-time, or as supplemental income. With the World Wide Web, magazines, newspapers, television, radio, advertising, marketing, public relations and publishing – there are many oceans of opportunity out there for creative non-fiction writers.

Creative non-fiction is the type of writing that people like Truman Capote, Guy Talese, Joan Didion, Tom Wolfe, John McPhee and Hunter S. Thompson made famous. It's the type of writing where the research is rich and multi-layered, the writing is dramatic and literary, you can take several points of view and have more freedom than with traditional journalism – or you can choose to stick to "just the facts" with a sprinkle of imagination for garnish.

It differs from traditional journalism in that you don't always have to take an objective stance in the research, reporting and writing. What you read in the front pages of newspapers is traditional journalism in democratic nations. Reporters and editors have a written rule to deliver "just the facts, ma'am."

The key element with this type of journalism is that you can be creative, but still tell the truth. It gives you the chance to be more of an artist with your writing, while still protecting the craft of journalism.

However you would like to get your stories across, you have now entered the world of story-tellers. This ebook is meant to prepare you not only in becoming a better writer and story-teller, but to become a professional one as well by getting your work published.

Good stories like the ones you will come up with have no use to anyone if they're stuck in a shoebox under your bed. Good stories need to see the light – they need to be published. You're not doing anyone any favours by hiding away your talent. I will present you with many avenues to see your stories published in various venues – it's up to you to make it happen. By going through all the chapters of this ebook, doing the assignments and lots of reading in your free time – you too can join the ranks of the great writers I've mentioned.

Chapter Breakdown

In the first chapter you will learn about the six major forms of creative non-fiction writing: memoir, personal essay, features, profiles, travel writing, analysis and reviews. The second chapter will discuss story-telling basics – how to tell a story with the BME theory (beginning, middle, end), inverted pyramid and the circle.

Next, some of the most important elements in making your stories fantastic will be explored – story ideas, research and interviewing. We'll discuss everything about how to make the best use out of story ideas, the library, and the Internet to get content.

To keep your reputation as a budding writer as clean as a cat throughout your career, chapter four is about journalism ethics and the laws surrounding publishing. These are the things you need to know to keep yourself out of trouble and to keep your editors wanting to work with you.

With that, we'll get into the heart of what makes a story great – voice, structure, description and narration. This chapter will be loads of fun.

Your story would not be yours without narration. We'll discuss points of view and the different perspectives you can take as a writer to deliver your narration in a well-crafted story.

Chapter Seven will discuss interviewing techniques and how important they are to making your story move from good to outstanding.

I'm not the funniest person on the planet, but I try to make the times I do tell a joke good ones. Humour is an important element to stories and is sometimes called for in lighter pieces. Chapter Eight will discuss how to best use humour and satire in your pieces and how to keep it tasteful (unless your intent is to write without taste).

Organization is the key to getting anything done. Chapter Nine will improve your skills in organizing your time as a writer and tips on how to balance your work life and professional life. In How To Write Creative Non-fiction, I want you all to be successful writers, but I want you to be well-balanced too.

Writing for visual and auditory media is an art form in itself – however that will be covered in another book – look out for it. There is work that can be had at your local community radio or television station if you know how to write for the eyes and the ears. In Chapter Ten we will look at tips on how to use these devices in more traditional forms of journalism, or perhaps maybe not so traditional – like writing for the Internet so you can entertain the reader through all of his or her senses.

When you present material to an editor or a publisher, it should be the cleanest copy it can be – clean meaning free from grammatical or spelling errors. Chapter Eleven will give you tips on how to become your own editor. These are tools that could make you an editor yourself.

One of the most important parts of this ebook is Chapter Twelve. You will learn about publishing markets, writing query letters, doing market research for your story ideas and getting your work into the hands of an editor for publication.

Since we don't live in a perfect world where people say "yes" to us all the time – this section will also deal with how to handle rejection – how to pick yourself up and keep trying after you've received a rejection slip, email or call. I once got an email that said something along the lines that life is about falling down seven times and getting up eight.

With all the knowledge you will acquire from this ebook, the final chapter, section Thirteen, will be your final assignment. This assignment will bring together everything you've learnt in the ebook and allow you to work with your new found knowledge to create dynamic and interesting non-fiction pieces of writing. After you've completed your final assignment, you're free to share them with me by sending me an email at: dkakonge@sympatico.ca, dkakonge@gmail.com or kakonged@yahoo.ca. You can find more information about my email address and how to contact me on my website: www.donnakakonge.com.

There are also many assignments in this book, other than the final one, I would like to have the chance to review and you can get the opportunity to share them with the world. You may want to consider starting a website from www.myspace.com and posting some of your work from this book. Just e-mail me and I'll take a look at your work for review. MySpace.com is free and will help you to fully enjoy the nature of this book. I have a MySpace.com space too at: www.myspace.com/donnakakonge.

It's going to be an exciting journey and one that you can take at any pace you wish. Remember that although writing can be a solitary practice, you're not alone. Many people are reading this ebook along with you all over the world and there will be a virtual community of people all learning to turn what they love – writing – into a living.

What I can guarantee you will be getting from me is a person with more than twenty one years of experience in journalism, teaching and writing. I've worked for Canada's public broadcaster, international broadcasters, magazines all over the world, for the Canadian government, as well as on community projects. I have a Bachelor of Journalism degree from Canada's best traditional school of journalism, Carleton University. I also have a Master's of Arts in media studies from Concordia University in Montreal. I am a PhD Candidate at OISE/University of Toronto and a law student at the University of London International Programmes online.

My teaching credentials include Carleton University, Makerere University in Kampala, Uganda (Africa's first and oldest university), Concordia University, Institute Linguistique Provincial, Sullivan Language Learning Center, Centennial College, Seneca College, Humber College, Guelph-Humber University and the University of Toronto. One of the courses I teach at the University of Toronto is Self-Publishing Around The World. I'm also the ebook author of What happened to the Afro? and many more that can be purchased through online stores such as Lulu.com, Amazon, iBookstore, Barnes & Noble, Kobo and Chapters/Indigo.

My future pursuits are to keep working hard as a journalist, writer, teacher and law – striving for an ideal blend to my traditional and non-traditional educational and professional background.

You can find out more about my other books and stories by visiting www.donnakakonge.com. You can buy the How To Talk To Crazy People book at: http://www.lulu.com/spotlight/kakonged?searchTerms=How+To+Talk+To+Crazy+People. My next book will be released September 2013 called Three Quarters to be self-published.

Okay....let's start!

CHAPTER 1

FORMS OF NON-FICTION WRITING

Welcome to your first chapter! As you go through each chapter you will be asked to complete optional assignments. While it is impossible for me to police you as you are completing these assignments, it is in your best interest as a writer to complete them. Most of your betterment as a writer will come through the completion of these short assignments. Similarly, at the end of most of our chapters, you'll be asked to complete a final chapter assignment. These assignments are also optional but I will be reviewing these ones, so make sure you take the time to complete them and you don't simply rush to the next chapter. Remember, there are no timelines, so take your time and complete a chapter and all the chapter assignments before moving on to the next chapter. The only semi-mandatory assignment is the final assignment which will also be reviewed and critiqued by me if you wish.

In summary

1) Each chapter has small optional assignments (not reviewed by me, but extremely helpful for progressing as a writer). You will see these throughout the ebook each being labeled as a **"mid-chapter assignment"**

2) Most chapters have a final assignment which you can upload to your own personal website if you wish. If you submit your assignments on the weekend – you can email me to take a look at it.

3) Successful completion of the ebook depends on the completion of a final assignment at the end of the ebook. This assignment is more complex and lengthy than the other assignments and will be reviewed by me.

Now, let's talk about writing...

Memoir Writing

A good example of memoir writing can be found in your own journals or diaries. Think of the *Diary of Anne Frank* as a perfect example. A young Jewish girl tells her story of growing up during WWII. Along the same lines, think of *Night* by Elie Wiesel. An older Jewish man tells his story of growing up during WWII and the devastation it brought to his family.

You don't need to go through a war to write your memoir. Cecil Foster's Island Wings is a more comfortable tale of his life in the Caribbean. However, many of you may be living in war-like situations, have unusual stories to tell, have an extremely interesting family, have no family at all – there are so many situations you may live. Writing a memoir is about telling the tales of your life. Your life story is as unique as we are individuals.

Here is an overview of the steps in creating a good memoir:

1. Defining emotional truth vs. factual truth
2. Answering the "so what" factor in a positive way – why are you writing this?
3. Methods of retrieving memory
4. Choosing your story-telling styles
5. Defining what the story is really all about
6. Avoiding the shopping list type of narrative
7. Avoiding the predictable
8. Understanding the universal is also the particular

Details and examples on the above steps are provided below....read on!

Step one: Defining emotional truth vs. factual truth

From Writers Digest online (www.writersdigest.com) Mimi Schwartz suggests eight keys to writing a good memoir in the article "From Memory to Memoir." The first tip is emotional truth vs. factual truth. Schwartz quotes from Joan Didion who writes about her experiences during a New England summer in "On Keeping a Notebook":

....perhaps it never did snow that August in Vermont; perhaps there never were flurries in the night wind, and maybe no one else felt the ground hardening and summer already dead even as we pretended to bask in it, but that was how it felt to me, and it might as well have snowed, could have snowed, did snow.

In the above excerpt, Didion is contrasting her emotional truth and the factual truth. Didion writes about her memories about how she felt that August in Vermont, not about what actually happened. There may be many moments of these types of experiences in your own writing through memoir.

An emotional truth is knowledge coming from your heart. It may not be accurate about past events, however, it *feels* true. It is indeed a truth because it was the way you were or still feel about a particular incident, yet there may not be any factual basis to your feelings.

For example, you may want to include in your memoir about your first car. It may feel to you that it was the "best car in the world." However, it may have been a Russian Lada like mine was and is probably one of the worst cars ever made.

This brings us to the factual truth. The truth is I had a Russian Lada – it was white, a stick-shift with a black and blue stripe in the middle of the car. It got me from A to B, didn't go fast so I didn't have to worry about speeding tickets even when I floored it. It is true that it is probably one of the worst cars ever made. However, my emotional truth is it was one of the best cars I ever had.

Emotional truth is something that is still valid in a memoir. With the same principles of traditional journalism, the best way to go is to include a fair balance of emotional truth and factual truth in your memoir. Ultimately, the decision is yours and you could decide to only include factual truth for a story about your mission to cover the Iraq war, for example. However, the writing would have more depth with the added touches of emotional truths as well.

MID-CHAPTER ASSIGNMENT 1.1 (don't forget, these are optional, non-graded assignments, but it is in your own best interest to complete them and share your work on your own personal websites)

Think of one memory from your past. Write down first your emotional truth about this memory, and then write the factual truth. The entire exercise should be about half a page. Below is an example of a memory I have of my younger years.

Example: An example of one of my earliest and clearest memories is seeing my Mom on a beach in St. Vincent & the Grenadines wearing a blue and white checkered bathing suit. She stood out from the beachgoers simply due to the size of the smile on her face during that day. I remember the waves crashing against the white sandy shore and I distinctly remember hearing the beautiful music the ocean makes when it crashes up against the ocean swimmers. The sounds of crashing waves mixed with youthful cries of joy.

Post your assignment to your personal website.

Step Two: Answering the "So What?" Factor in a Positive Way – Why are You Writing This?

The second tip for memoir writing, according to Schwartz is what she calls the "so what?" factor. This is the assumption many writers fall into that no one would care to hear about their life. Many writers may suffer from problems with esteem, not understanding their stories are special and unique because everyone is special and unique. However, Schwartz offers this example from Pat Hampl's description of taking piano chapters from "Memory and Imagination":

> When I was seven, my father, who played the violin on Sundays with a nicely tortured flair which we considered artistic, led me by the hand down a long, unlit corridor in St. Luke's School basement, a sort of tunnel that ended in a room full of pianos. There many little girls and a single sad boy were playing truly tortured scales and arpeggios in a mash of troubled sound. My father gave me over to Sister Olive Marie, who did look remarkable like an olive.

In this example, the "so what?" factor is answered by a resounding "so wonderful." The writing brings us directly into Hampl's life as a young girl and perhaps since many of us have been through similar situations, we can relate. It is the fact as we encounter strangers and loved ones where we tell stories they may not have heard – we can often find "ourselves." When that happens, you can have your reader hooked. You draw them in and you need not worry about the "so what?" factor – you find your answer through a common bond.

An example of a bad "so what" factor – something that perhaps no one would care about would be a shopping list style of writing from your journal.

I went to the store, picked up some milk and cereal, and then prepared breakfast at home. I flicked on the TV and watched all the morning talk shows. I had lunch, watched the afternoon soaps, went for a walk, and then went to bed.

The above is the kind of thing you want to avoid. It is natural most readers would say a resounding "so what?" to this type of narrative.

Discovering what is unique about your story and answering the "so what?" factor starts with asking yourself some important questions. Here are some to get you started, all centred around finding what makes you unique before you start to write your memoir.

- What's your favourite breakfast meal?
- Do you prefer working in the day, evening or night?
- Do you have pets?
- What's your favourite colour?
- Do you speak other languages than your mother tongue?
- What's your dream job?
- What do you tend to dream about at night? What do you daydream?
- What are your nightmares? What do you worry about?
- Do you have siblings?
- What's your favourite room in your home?
- Do you prefer paper or a computer screen or both?
- What's your earliest and clearest memory?
- Do you have a significant other and how do you feel about s/he?
- Who's your favourite celebrity?
- What's your favourite movie? Television show? Radio Show?
- What's your favourite website?
- Who's your best friend?
- What gets you through the day?

- What are your religious beliefs?
- Who do you vote for?

These are just samples of some questions aimed at getting to the core of what makes you special. The important thing to note when you're asking yourself the above questions is to ask yourself why? Why are you the way you are? Who or whom have been the important people to shape your life?

MID-CHAPTER ASSIGNMENT 1.2

Write a one-page autobiography of yourself using the questions above to help determine how you are unique. Dig deep to discover the most unique parts of yourself. Post your assignment to your personal website.

You want to start the story with a beginning, middle and an end. Typically in this type of story structure, which will be explained more later, the middle is basically the climax, or turning point of the story.

The assignment should be no more than a one thousand words and focus on a powerful part of your life that seems symbolic of the most important chapter you've learnt.

We'll move onto step three.

Step Three: Methods of Retrieving Memory

The third point Schwartz mentions is retrieving memory. There are many things you can do to bring your memory to near-perfect recall.

For things which have happened recently, most of the time there are no problems in remembering information that would add to your memoir. However for more distant events, you may have to draw upon photo albums, ask family members and friends, actually go back to that grade four classroom, visit the old house – whatever needs to be done to tell your story.

Hampl used these methods to recall the piano chapter:

When I reread what I had written just after I finished it, I realized that I had told a number of lies. I think it was my father who took me to meet my teacher – but maybe he only took me to meet my teacher and there was no actual chapter that day. And do I even know that he played the violin – didn't he take up his violin again much later, as a result of my piano playing, and not the reverse...More: Sister Olive Marie did sneeze in the sun, but was her name Olive?

Again, you'll notice that the above statement touches once more on the subject of emotional vs. factual truth. The key to writing a good memoir if this is what you would like is to start by keeping a journal. If you already do this – great – you're one step ahead. If you don't, it's not too late to catch up, however, if you have children whom you would like to see make writing part of their lives – encourage them to keep a journal as well.

Try to spend as much available time you have each day writing down the day's events, your thoughts and basically keeping a log of your life. Nowadays, many people even do this online and it's become extremely popular to read what is known as "blogs." We are going to have you start your own blog in an upcoming chapter and writing creative non-fiction for the Internet.

Julia Cameron in *The Right to Write*, also the author of *The Artist Within*, suggests that people who want to write keep what she calls "morning pages." This involves getting up in the morning and writing in a style that Virginia Wolfe made famous called "stream of consciousness." This involves completely uncensored writing – just putting down all your thoughts.

If some of you are like me and find it hard to write long-hand as fast as you think – try typing your words and keeping the notes on your computer. This way, you can come back to structure and edit the material later.

MID-CHAPTER ASSIGNMENT 1.3

This is an assignment on prompting your memory recall.

Look at one of your older pictures and try to remember the events of that day or month. Try to remember what the weather was like. Try to remember the events in the world happening on that day. Try and remember any friends that you had then that you don't have now or still have. Did you dress differently? Were your political views different?

For this assignment I want you to write a short one page or less on the person who you were then. It can include everything from a physical description to your philosophical standpoints. Try and capture the true essence of who you used to be and upload your assignment to your personal website.

We'll move onto the fourth step.

Step Four: Choosing Your Story-telling Styles

Schwartz continues with her analysis of memoir writing by making the fourth point storytelling choices:

> You can tell the same story in more than one way. A disastrous weekend, for example, may be told as tragedy or comedy, depending on how you feel about the material – and that may change over time. Family considerations are also a factor. If you have to live with the people you are writing about, it's hard to say, "I made that up. That's not you!" when their names are the same. That's why many writers, like Pam Houston, avoid memoir on delicate subjects, saying, "I write fiction to tell the truth."
>
> Fear of censure, however, can also be an imaginative trigger in memoir, helping to expand your perspective. You may portray the father you hate with more complexity, for example, thinking about what your mother, who loved him, will say.
>
> More often, fear of censure can seduce you into Hallmark Card writing: "My father is my hero. Never a harsh word, never a bad piece of advice. I love him 100%, always have, always will...." Nice, but suspect. Human relations are complex; fathers are not like in "The Brady Bunch" – not every day, anyway.

Tragedy and Comedy:

This source comes from http://everything2.com.
In Marlowe's Doctor Faustus, Faustus wrestles with his mission in life, and what he wants to do for a living. He turns down medicine, as he can only prolong the inevitable. He turns down theology and the church because if all men are sinners, no matter what, what good does it do to worship and work to that end when he must fail in the end? Lastly, Faustus wrestles with science, but this too is faulty in his eye, because there is only finite amount information to learn in the world. So Faustus turns to alchemy and signs a contract with Mephistopheles, one of the devil's "henchmen", for lack of a better word. In the end, Faustus is told that to be released from his 20 year contract and go to heaven eternally in stead of hell, he just must ask God for forgiveness; however, Faustus can not understand nor accept how anyone, let alone God could forgive a man such as he who turned his back on him previously, so in the end, Faustus is dragged to Hell for all time, because he could not humble himself and ask forgiveness of a greater being.

Tragedy is not just a sad story, because that is simply sad, or unfortunate. This is my definition, which is not necessarily the correct one. This definition deals mainly with tragedy in literature.

Tragedy is when a character creates his or her personal and moral downfall and destruction of self and/or life that results from a single, limiting decision chosen with the understanding of other possible choices but with the feeling of having no choice, so that the character is left only to follow a choice that ends up in the character's downfall. The character feels that they have no choice because of the extent of their environment that has affected them, rather than an innate flaw in their character. It is because the character understands that they have the choices but believe so firmly that they have none and this result in destruction, that there is tragedy. The character also does not believe that they are responsible for their choices and actions, because the can only perceive one choice of action. This idea also evokes a feeling of empathy and astonishment from the reader because they are able to perceive that the character could have had a way out if they were not so intent on their purpose. With the end tending to result in unnecessary or sorrowful death or the character left with out resolution, the tragedy is experienced by the reader.

Comedy on the other hand is something which arouses amusement or makes you laugh. If in the above example Faustus fate was be turned into a goat rather than go to hell, this is something that can arouse amusement and would turn the story into more of a comedy.

We'll now move onto step five.

Step Five: Defining What the Story is Really All About

The fifth point Schwartz mentions is "What is this really about?" The fact something happened is not the only reason to write. It needs to amount to something. With the exclusion of a diary (although journals can make great sources for your writing) you still want to draw the reader into your story. You still want to include the important elements of journalism: Who, What, Where, When, Why and How.

This is something Mary Morris did when she wrote about her trip to the Great Wall of China to the Berlin Wall. She made sure the reader was actually on the trip with her:

> The dining car looked more like a Chinese laundry than a restaurant – noisy, frenzied, boiling hot. Warm Chinese beer was being handed out and I grabbed one from the passing tray as everyone else seemed to do. The car was packed and I saw no seats, but then Pierre, the French saxophone player I'd met at the Mongolian embassy, waved me across the room, pointing to half a seat. "So," he said, putting an arm around my shoulder, "you made it."

The focus statement keeps you on a fairly even path in your writing. Rather than randomly telling stories that could give the impression of a series of non-fiction short stories that do not have a link – a focus helps to link your stories and give them purpose.

Here's an example of a focus from the back cover of a biography called *Nelson Mandela* by Mary Benson published in 1986:

> Imprisoned since 1962, Nelson Mandela has become a legend in his own lifetime; the embodiment of the struggle for liberation in South Africa and a vital

symbol of a new society. As the international campaign for his release grows, he and his wife, Winnie, continue to triumph over unremitting persecution.

In this timely and absorbing biography, Mary Benson describes Mandela's life, work and ideas from his childhood in the royal family of the Thembu people to his membership and eventual leadership of the African National Congress. Her book sheds important light on the man whose release is widely regarded as the essential first step towards averting catastrophe in that tragic land.

Now here's an assignment for you.

MID-CHAPTER ASSIGNMENT 1.4

To get to the heart of what the point of your memoir would be – write a half a page focus statement which summarizes your story, including the word "because."

As a quick example: "I'm alive today because of the loving nature of my parents and siblings. They have been the true soldiers of armour in keeping me out of harm's way."

That is a focus statement. The rest of your story would centre on that statement of truth. Upload your focus statement to your personal website.

The next step is six.

Step Six: Avoiding the Shopping List Type of Narrative

Schwartz's sixth point is to beware of the shopping-list narrative. She suggests a good exercise I will have you do for this section on memoir.

Mid-Chapter Assignment 1.5

I would like you now to complete a short assignment. This assignment will not be graded but it will allow you to practice the skills you've learnt above. This assignment will have you summarize your life in six pages. Make sure it's stimulating. Here's an example from one of Schwartz's students, Nicole Ross:

We all have stories, I think, and the stories we tell are carefully chosen. There's the story in which I dance on the table, am witty beyond belief, and everyone wants me. I'm also wearing a slinky black dress and fishnets. That's the one I tell to attractive guys who look at me a certain way. There there's the story I tell to my conservative grandparents about the latest fraternity party I went to – minus the alcohol, the cops in the bushes, and the dark-skinned guy looped in chains and reeking of Coolwater....

Upload your assignment to your personal website.

Step Seven: The seventh point Schwartz mentions is to avoid the predictable. Ultimately, you need to ask the question, "What is unexpected in my story?"

A good example of this comes from Frank McCourt's *Angela's Ashes*, where the man is a drunk, spending all his money on booze, but he still loves his family:

He staggered to me and hugged me and I smelled the drink I used to smell in America. My face was wet from his tears and his spit and his snot and I was hungry and I didn't know what to say when he cried all over my head.

With this story, it becomes more than just a dead-beat Dad story.

You want to make sure you're including the aspects of your story that make it unique. A lot of knowledge in this area comes from reading widely and especially other memoirs. By reading the good ones out there you will discover a keen sense of what makes a memoir great.

You may have experience of telling stories about your life to others and discovering from their reactions what aspects were unique to your life circumstances. Use this information to include in your memoir.

Step eight: The universal is in the particular

The final point Schwartz mentions is "the universal is in the particular":

"We ate our Christmas meal and were happy and content" is bland compared to "We ate our Christmas goose stuffed with Nana's chestnuts and laughed at Uncle Al who kept cracking walnuts, making shells fly across the room like missiles." It is the particular that carries us back into the past, allowing us to connect small moments and see larger meanings. Through the particular, we also discover the imaginative powers that transform fact into artifact, factual truths into emotional truths, memory into memoir. A surprise word or image appears, and suddenly we see our third grade teacher in her silky, turquoise blouse and hear the exact conversation, without a tape recorder, of the young saxophonist on the train to Berlin.

Best of all, we can gain ride the Queens Metropolitan Bus in ripped jodhpurs and a bloody knee, like the old days.

There was a time in publishing when many people who did not traditionally publish books were locked out of the market because they were told their writing and their stories were not "universal" enough. That is changing widely with the likes of Toni Morrison, Zadie Smith, Salmon Rushdie and Wole Soyinka to name a few who are publishing widely.

A universal concept in writing means aspects of a story which every human on the universe can relate to. Stories about families for example, love; work, school, etc. are experiences the majority of the literate world knows.

Conversely, the particular is something which may be obscure to many readers – such as ancient rituals in Africa, India, China or Rome. These are experiences many humans living today may not know about – but, it doesn't mean they don't want to read about it because these books sell and sell well.

Memoir writing was in vogue in the late 1990s and it was in great demand from publishing houses. It's less popular now in terms of the type of writing that gets published. However, you will find that once you've been in the writing business long enough – everything that goes up comes down. As well, everything that is down goes up.

If you would love to write your memoir – I will help you work on that and if you search hard enough – you will find a market for your work.

Personal Essay

The personal essay form of non-fiction writing is popular. It differs from memoir writing because they tend to be shorter pieces that are publishable in magazines, newspapers and online, rather than in books like memoir writing.

This writing can also be known as the "I" form of writing. When I went to journalism school, it was a cardinal sin to use the "I" word in any of my copy. This was true for all students. Now, things have changed and many publications want a first-person account of a story.

These essays can take a variety of formats. You could be telling the story of delivering your first child, quitting smoking, your romance with your partner, or what it's like to grow up in Iran. As you can see, these essays can take on a variety of subjects and the ideas should come from you. Sometimes though, as we will discuss later, friends, family and strangers can inspire you with great ideas too.

Personal essays are a brave thing to do. You may find that with challenging subjects, like writing about your divorce, it brings up all kinds of emotions and feelings. One of the ethics of good creative non-fiction writing is to tell the truth. If something hurts, write it. You'll be surprised how many readers will respect your honesty and sympathize or relate. If your style is to remain more reserved with your emotions, write in a balanced way. Many readers will respect how well you have seemed to find solutions for your problems.

Your personality should come through in a personal essay. It's about speaking to the world in your voice through writing. A good editor will respect that.

Here's an example of a personal essay from www.linkup-parents.com. You can see from this format that knowing how to write a good personal essay can be helpful even with traditional college entrance essays:

Three times a week after school I go visit my dad. When I enter the hospital room where he has lain in a coma since his accident, my eyes often wander to the lone golf ball my mom placed at his bedside. Just six months ago, my father was driving a golf cart across the street that bisects the local golf choice when he was hit by a car. He suffered severe brain injury, and the doctors have ruled out any possibility of him waking up again. When I look at him lying in bed, frail but peaceful as if he were asleep, it's hard not to dwell on the "what ifs": what if he hadn't played golf that day? What if he hadn't been behind the fence when the black Camry plowed into it? What if I still had the chance to ask all those questions that choke me up when I see him in the hospital? I can't pretend that I have developed enough distance from the event to draw conclusions about life, but I am already beginning to see myself in very different terms.

(** instructor's comments: Notice the use of the universal in the particular above.)

Ironically, through this accident my dad has given a chance to face reality head-on. Before the accident, my relationship with him was warm but fraught with tension. He never seemed satisfied with what I did and reprimanded me for every wrong step I took. He had strong opinions about my hairstyle, clothes, friends, and--above everything else--my academic performance. When I was not sitting at my desk in my room, he invariably asked me why I had nothing to do and told me I should not procrastinate. He stressed that if I missed my teenage years of studying, I would regret it later. He didn't like me going out with my friends, so I often ended up staying at home--I was never allowed to sleep over at other students' homes. All I remember from my past high school years is going to school and coming back home. I was confused by my parents' overprotective attitude, because they emphasized independence yet never actually gave me a chance to be independent.

In terms of career, my dad often lectured me about which ones are acceptable and which are not. He worried incessantly about whether I would ever get into college, and he often made me feel as if he would never accept my choices. Rather than standing up for myself, I simply assumed that if I studied hard, he would no longer be disappointed in me. Although I tried hard, I never seemed to get it quite right; he always found fault with something. As if that weren't enough, he frequently compared me to my over-achieving older brother, asking me why I couldn't be more like him. I must admit that at times I even questioned whether my dad really loved me. After all, he never expressed admiration for what I did, and my attempts to impress him were always in vain.

(** Instructors comments: This story becomes much more interesting when the complexities of this human relationship are explored. When you start reading the essay you don't think they author would write anything critical of his father who is a coma. However, this story takes shape because it's unpredictable and complex)

In retrospect, I don't think I fully understood what he was trying to tell me. These days, when I come home to an empty house, it strikes me just how dependent on my parents' care and support I have been so far. Now that my dad is in the hospital and my mom is always working, I see that I must develop the strength to stand alone one day. And, for the very first time, I now realize that this is exactly what my dad was trying to make me see. I understand that he had a big heart, even though he didn't always let it show; he was trying to steer me in the right direction, emphasizing the need to develop independence and personal strength. He was trying to help me see the world with my own eyes, to make my own judgments and decide for myself what I would eventually become. When my dad was still with us, I took all of his advice the wrong way. I should not have worried so much about living up to my parents' expectations; their only expectation of me, after all, is that I be myself.

In mapping out my path to achieving my independence, I know that education will allow me to build on the foundations with which my parents have provided me. My academic interests are still quite broad, but whereas I was once frustrated by my lack of direction, I am now excited at the prospect of exploring several fields before focusing on a particular area. Strangely, dealing with my father's accident has made me believe that I can tackle just about any challenge. Most importantly, I am more enthusiastic about my education than ever before. In embarking on my college career, I will be carrying with me my father's last gift and greatest legacy: a new desire to live in the present and the confidence to handle whatever the future might bring.

Here's is another example of a personal story essay that fits into the area of creative non-fiction:

I walked into the first class that I have ever taught and confronted utter chaos. The four students in my Latin class were engaged in a heated spitball battle. They were all following the lead of Andrew, a tall eleven-year-old African-American boy.

(**Notice in the very first sentence conflict is introduced. This helps grab the reader's attention. Although the last essay was great, it was started off very poorly. We will speak very shortly on constructing good starting sentences).

Andrew turned to me and said, "Why are we learning Latin if no one speaks it? This a waste of time."

I broke out in a cold sweat. I thought, "How on Earth am I going to teach this kid?"

It was my first day of Summerbridge, a nationwide collaborative of thirty-six public and private high schools. Its goal is to foster a desire to learn in young, under-privileged students, while also exposing college and high-school students to teaching. Since I enjoy tutoring, I decided to apply to the program. I thought to myself, "Teaching can't be that difficult. I can handle it." I have never been more wrong in my life.

After what seemed like an eternity, I ended that first class feeling as though I had accomplished nothing. Somehow I needed to catch Andrew's attention. For the next two weeks, I tried everything from indoor chariot races to a Roman toga party, but nothing seemed to work.

During the third week, after I had exhausted all of my ideas, I resorted to a game that my Latin teacher had used. A leader yells out commands in Latin and the students act out the commands. When I asked Andrew to be the leader, I found the miracle that I had been seeking. He thought it was great that he could order the teacher around with commands such as "jump in place" and "touch the window." I told him that if he asked me in Latin to do something, I would do it as long as he would do the same. With this agreement, I could teach him new words outside the classroom, and he could make his teacher hop on one foot in front of his friends. Andrew eventually gained a firm grasp of Latin.

Family night occurred during the last week of Summerbridge. We explained to the parents what we had accomplished. At the conclusion, Andrew's mom thanked me for teaching him Latin. She said, "Andrew wanted to speak Latin with someone, so he taught his younger brother."

My mouth fell open. I tempered my immediate desire to utter, "Andrew did what?" I was silent for a few seconds as I tried to regain my composure, but when I responded, I was unable to hide my surprise.

Here's another example of a Toronto-based essay from a book called *Utopia: Towards a New Toronto*, edited by Jason McBride and Alana Wilcox. The book is a collection of essays on how to make Toronto, Canada a better place. This excerpt comes from Philip Evans:

Rooftops, fence, trees, grass, sidewalk, grass, pavement, median, occasionally varied by discarded artifacts of clothing such as the all-too-familiar lone shoe, garbage of all sorts thrown from car windows and, of choices, roadkill: the greater part of my teenage years was spent staring down at the sidewalk.

Like many Toronto suburbs, Brampton had an isolating quality for a resentful not-yet-old-enough-to-drive thirteen-year-old whose understanding of relentless housing farms was limited to an endless matrix of sidewalks. I remember counting 1,023 concrete sidewalk pavers on my way to school. After cutting through the catwalk at the end of my street, it was a thirty-minute stroll to school along a four-lane road of commuters. This was hardly a shared experience. On the way, there was a 7-Eleven where I could enjoy a moment of perceived freedom while sipping a cream-soda slurpee and kicking a pop can as long as I could. The community offered a pedestrian few features beyond these. Most of the time, I stared down at the sidewalk and drifted into my thoughts.

Developing a great opening:

I had a terrific professor when I was doing my undergraduate work at Carleton University named Dr. Catherine McKercher. The class she taught was in-depth reporting.

One of the most important things I learned from that class was how to develop a great opening for any story – which also applies to personal essays.

The tip she taught me is when you're writing, every sentence should be complete within itself, but at the same time raising a question. This is the most important thing about the opening sentence. After that, you, the writer, must concentrate on answering the questions raised by the following sentences, as well as raising new questions to keep the reader on your side. This may sound odd, but the best way to demonstrate this is to use an example:

> I waited for the bus for 20 minutes to head to my destination. Once the bus showed up I noticed it had the number 40 on it and remembered I was heading to 940 Lansdowne Ave. I was on my way for my first day of work.

You'll see from this short example that the first sentence raises the question of where am I going? Also note, the sentence is still complete. The second and third sentences answer the question raised in the first sentence, but still leave room for more interesting writing because the reader still hasn't discovered the type of work I'm doing.

While all sentences are important, none is more important than you're opening sentence. You need to grab the reader's attention immediately. You can do this by adding suspense, shocking them, or asking questions they too want answered. In the classic novel "Notes From Underground" Dostoevsky surprises and shocks his readers by having his first person narrator speak very lowly of themselves. He starts his novel with the following few sentences "I am a sick man...I am a spiteful man. I am an unpleasant man. I think my liver is diseased."

In another example, the book "Complicated Kindness" by Miriam Toews starts off with the following opening.

"I live with my father, Ray Nickel, in that low brick bungalow out on the highway number twelve. Blue shutters, brown door, one shattered window. Nothing great. The furniture keeps disappearing, though. That keeps things interesting."

As you can see, these opening few sentences help grab your attention and make you want to keep reading. Make sure when you are drafting your non-fiction writing pieces that you use the same methods to help create interest in your non-fiction pieces.

Conclusion

The personal essay is a shorter form of writing than the memoir style discussed earlier. In a personal essay, you can concentrate on a subject, an issue, express your opinions, etc. and it all comes from your personal point of view.

Memoir is different because as you're telling the story of your life, it may involve many different characters and is based on aspects or a particular situation in your life. It's "life writing," your life. A personal essay is similar to the types of essays you may have had to do in school but from your viewpoint.

MID-CHAPTER ASSIGNMENT 1.6

Below is an assignment to help you practice your skills with the personal essay format: This essay is not marked, but to complete it will help you to become a much better non-fiction writer.

- Write a personal essay on your feelings towards the city or town you are currently living in. Describe the city or town as if it were a person. What characteristic does it posses? How has it helped you become who you are today? What are its weaknesses?

Your assignment should be about one page in length. When you've completed it upload it to your personal website.

Features

These stories give you the chance to explore some of your areas of interest. Whether it is sports, popular culture, entertainment, community work, international development, science and technology, cars, etc. – you can write a story that will feature your interests.

One of the most important things most writers believe is to "write what you know." Traditional journalists are often writing about things they may not know a lot about, but the good ones have done their research and still churned out a story on tight deadlines.

You don't have to be an expert before writing a feature – the research tips I will teach you will help you become one before you start writing. Here are some examples to inspire you from William E. Blundell's *The Art and Craft of Feature Writing*. This example comes from George Getschow in a 1980 piece on immigration from Mexico:

NAPIZARO, Mexico – An astonishingly effective U.S. trade program is operating in this rural hamlet of 1,200 people – but Uncle Sam knows nothing about it. He wouldn't like it if he did.

Napizaro has street lights, new brick homes with TV antennas sprouting from their rooftops, a modern community center and infirmary, and a new bullring name "North Hollywood California." It is a fitting name. The money for the bullring and all the rest came from North Hollywood in exchange for Napizaro's main export: its male population.

For decades this town has systematically sent its men north to work as illegal aliens in small plants and businesses in the California community, and for decades they have sent their pay home, part t earmarked for civic improvements.

"Our town is a monument to our workers. None of this would be possible without them," says Augustin Campos, a 61-year-old town elder and an early migrant himself. It was Mr. Campos's success in North Hollywood (the first year he went thereto work he earned $4,000, or more than all the Napizaro villagers combined) that attracted all the others North Hollywood, where they now work in a number of factories, including one started by a Napizaro villager.

The price of the new-found prosperity is high. Napizaro is a town of children, old men and lonely women. More than tree-quarters its 156 heads of household are in the States, and they return only briefly for the town festival in January if they can come home at all. After many years of such separation, they will finally return for good to houses built with their savings, some of them stunning homes with landscaped courtyards and even saunas. "The boys want nice places to retire to," Mr. Campos says. In Mexico, a nice place to retire to can be built for $8,000.

Napizaros's wealth is an anomaly in poverty-stricken rural Mexico. It stems from the town's unusual system of self-taxation and the willingness its men to spend so much of their lives away from their village. But the extent its migration is no anomaly. It is the norm. Pushed by poverty, pulled by the lure of jobs that pay at least 10 times what they can make here, men throughout rural Mexico are going north in numbers that may even exceed the highest estimates, about five million crossings a year, with some men making several crossings in the book of a year.

A journey through central Mexico shows town after town almost stripped of working-age males much of the year. In a country that on the whole can't create enough jobs for its people, so great has the rural migration become that farm fields lie untended and local businesses suffer severe labor shortages. Now some skilled workers from the cities, lured by U.S. pay scales, are joining the northern migration too.

The story goes on in more depth, but this gives you a sense of all the research and writing that goes into doing feature articles. Before we get to research, we'll discuss another area of creative non-fiction writing – profiles – just before you do an assignment.

MID-CHAPTER ASSIGNMENT 1.7

This assignment will have you complete a feature assignment on Honduras. It is one of the poorest countries in Central America, but also one of the most beautiful. It also suffers through one of the worlds worst AIDS outbreaks. I would like you to write a featured article on the country but you're able to focus on whatever element you wish. For example you could write it from a tourist standpoint; you could write about the AIDS problem, you could write about poverty, the culture, and food and so on.

Before you start writing however you need to research your topic. Feel free to use whatever sources you wish, but here are a few to get you started.

http://www.billstephenson.co.uk/bs_HTM%20PAGES/HONDURASINTRO.HTM - explores the AIDS problem through pictures *** There is some nudity on this site

http://sidewalkmystic.com/Why_Honduras_Tourism.htm - Some information on visiting Honduras

https://.cia.gov/cia/publications/factbook/geos/ho.html - CIA fact book. Information on history, politics, economy and map.

Your feature story should be about two pages long, have a sufficient title and a clear point of view. Don't forget to complete a focus statement before starting this piece.

Once you are done, upload your work to your personal website. Good luck!

Profiles

Usually the type of profiles many magazines are looking for include ones on the "rich and the famous." If you could get a story on what Janet Jackson is up to lately, chances are you'll find someone to publish your work.

However, there are many avenues to get profiles on "regular" people doing extraordinary things published. Such as, an educated pizza-maker, a doctor whom is the owner of twin dogs, a woman that lives on an island alone, etc. You get the idea.

Profiles can also be done on people who have ideas or are working on projects that help one person to everyone on the planet.

There is so much potential in what you could do as a profile, it's endless. Really, the best yardstick in measuring what to do is to ask this question: Does this person interest me? With a simple answer of "yes," you know you're on your way to writing a great profile.

Some of the best profiles written can be found in David Remnick's *Life Stories* which are a collection of profiles from *The New Yorker*. This is selection is from Mark Singer called "Secrets of the Magus." It's a profile on the world-famous magician Ricky Jay:

> The playwright David Mamet and the theatre director Gregory Mosher affirm that some years ago, late one night in the bar of the Ritz-Carlton Hotel in Chicago, this happened:
>
> Ricky Jay, who is perhaps the most gifted sleight-of-hand artist alive, was performing magic with a deck of cards. Also present was a friend of Mamet and Mosher's named Christ Nogulich, the director of food and beverage at the hotel. After twenty minutes of disbelief-suspending manipulations, Jay spread the deck face up on the bar counter and asked Nogulich to concentrate on a specific card but not to reveal it. Jay then assembled the deck face down, shuffled, cut it into two piles, and asked Nogulich to point to one of the piles and name his card.
>
> "Three of clubs," Nogulich said, and he was then instructed to turn over the top card.
>
> He turned over the three of clubs.

As you read, this is a great opening for a profile on Ricky Jay. The focus of the piece is on his experience as a magician and it opens with how skillful he is at his craft. The following paragraphs will give you a sense of how much work went into this article printed in the esteemed *New Yorker*:

> One morning last December, a few days before Christmas, Jay came to see me in my office. He wore a dark-gray suit and a black shirt that was open at the collar, and the colors seemed to match his mood. The most uplifting magic, Jay believes, has a spontaneous, improvisational vigor. Nevertheless, because he happened to be in New York we had made a date to get together, and I, invoking a journalistic imperative, had specifically requested that he come by my office and

do some magic while I took notes. He hemmed and hawed and then, reluctantly, consented. Though I had no idea what was in store, I anticipated being completely fooled.

At that point, I had known Jay for two years, during which we had discussed his theories of magic, his relationships with and opinions of other practioners of the art, his rigid opposition to public revelations of the techniques of magic, and his relentless passion for collecting rare books and manuscripts, art, and other artifacts connected to the history of magic, gambling, unusual entertainments, and frauds and confidence games.

Singer had spent at least two years researching this story and gathering facts and information to fully know Ricky Jay. This is the kind of thing that makes creative non-fiction far different from traditional journalism, where in daily news you may come across a source that you only speak with for five minutes for a "sound bite."

The most important thing to understand about writing a good profile is really getting to know your subject. Surface appearances add for colourful detail, but do not get to the heart of who a person really is.

Again, like I mentioned in the memoir exercise about digging for information to recall your memory – dig for information from your subject. If you have the time, take the time to get to know the person thoroughly so it's a well-rounded account of their life. Your job is to present this interesting person to the world – take that job seriously. Also, understand why you are telling this person's story. Are you trying to break stereotypes? Are you bringing to light fantastic achievements? Are you uncovering scandalous truths? Are you showing both sides and the kaleidoscope nature that many of us have as relatively complex individuals.

Also keep in mind these things:

- People will always try to show you their best sides – dig to know more
- People sometimes don't always remember all the details – be strategic with your questions
- Interview friends and family

With the above things in mind, it's also key to remember that when you're writing creative non-fiction for a magazine, newspaper or online – often you're restricted by length and word count. There's only so much you can do within a given page and word count – do your best and be fair!

Conclusion

Capturing a person's essence on paper is one of the most magical things you can do. Make every effort to be fair to your subject, as well as fair to yourself as the writer by making sure you're subject is coming clean with you.

MID-CHAPTER ASSIGNMENT 1.8

Take someone from your everyday life and write a profile about them of one to two pages in length and post it to your personal website.

Travel

Theodore A. Rees Cheney says in his book *Writing Creative Nonfiction* the difference between traditional travel writing and creative nonfiction travel writing is:

> They try their best to give us a vicarious sense of place – they give us its feel. The best travel writers also try to give us a feel for the place, but they don't consider their purpose literary.....their nonfiction writing is creative and entertaining as it informs. The traditional travel writer transports us; the creative travel writer speaks of transport (Cheney, 248-249).

Hopefully, this is understood. There are many examples of this form in the book if you can get a hold it.

Creative non-fiction travel writing can also take the form of travelogues. This is where a journal comes in handy again. You may have taken notes about a particular place and how it made you feel in the world. A travelogue gives more of your personal reflection, rather than from a descriptive perspective.

This example of a creative non-fiction travel piece comes from Heather Greenwood-Davis who also writes travel pieces for *The Toronto Star*. The piece is called "Desert Rose" and it appeared in the December 2005 issue of *Elle Canada*:

Where: this affluent United Arab Emirates city is a safe haven in the Middle East, enjoying good relations with its neighbours. With guaranteed sunshine, white, sandy beaches, international hotels and friendly locals, Dubai is a popular hot spot with Europeans.

Your guide: Canadian soprano Michelle Todd has performed at Ontario's Shaw Festival and Stage West. She represented Canada twice at the Cantai Festival in Taiwan with Ensemble Resonance before moving to Dubai five years ago. Internationally heralded for her acting and singing, Todd recently performed in Philadelphia and will appear in England, New York and Tokyo in 2006.

The vibe: with its mix of nationalities and religions, "Dubai is a very cosmopolitan place," says Todd. "Out of one million people, only about 18 percent are truly local." Tolerance is the mantra here: disrespect of a person's gender, religion, race or nationality is viewed as a hate crime. Dubai, an international business centre, is the most lenient city in the Middle East. While some local women choose to wear traditional long robes called abayas (often with Chanel underneath), many do not. Expats visitors are allowed to dress any way they like, although covering up bare skin is mandatory in mosques.

Big picture: "Dubai is really struggling with its identity," Todd says. "On the one hand, it's very modern; on the other hand, it desperately wants to hold on to its Arabic way of life." The result is nothing short of phenomenal, as the modern competes with the historic at every turn. The desert is minutes away from the high-tech downtown core, women in abayas shop alongside Gucci-clad fashionistas, and New World fusion cuisine is just as accessible as the traditional chicken shwarma and tabbouleh. Dubai is a city where the impossible is possible. If you can dream it, chances are it's already under construction there, like the world's tallest building or man-made islands in the shape of a palm tree. "The beauty of the architecture is highlighted by the art that is just as likely to be found on a street corner as in a museum," Todd adds.

In this example, more description is used for Dubai. With the vibrant language and vocabulary used, Greenwood-Davis has been able to help the reader visualize being in the city. This is something you would want to accomplish in your own writing.

Here's another example where in this one, the place is not as important as the action. The article talks about cycling holidays entitled "Tour de force." It comes from *The Toronto Star* and is written by Sue Lebrecht:

> Peter Wood remembers the day – and it wasn't that long ago – when people would show up for a cycling vacation in dress shoes and jeans, not even packing a helmet.
>
> "I remember one gentleman who would actually try to read a book while riding," says Wood, who is a guide with Freewheeling Adventures.
>
> But now that cycling has become a mainstream way to hit the road, "we don't' have any of that," says Wood, head guide for the Nova Scotia cycling excursions company that has seen a gearing up of business since it started offering tours around Atlantic Canada back in 1987, and now overseas.
>
> "People know what to wear and come prepared."

Although that's just the beginning of the piece, you can see that it discusses less about Nova Scotia and more about cycling and the equipment needed to ride. It's filled with quotes and expert opinions that will guide the reader, just as I am your writing tour guide.

More tips on travel writing

Keep in mind travel doesn't always have to mean boarding a plane, train or automobile to discover the great unknown. Sometimes you can discover that right where you live.

There might be an area of the city or town where you live you didn't know about. There might be a historical landmark that would make an amazing story. Get in the practice of reading those plaques you find so carefully placed on landmarks. You may discover something worth sharing with the rest of your community, nation or the world.

Travel is expensive and not everyone can afford it or place it as a priority – however they still like to write about interesting places. If there's a particular place you haven't been to you would like to see – or you've been there and don't remember it in detail – try contacting the consulate or embassy of the country and you may be able to write a story about a place based on the press material. Just make sure you're working with an editor who will make it clear in the piece you didn't actually visit the place, but these are things you find interesting about it.

As well, there is a good website that often has information for travel writers. You may be able to receive a paid trip in order to do your travel writing – just keep in mind this may colour your judgment of the place and you should state in the story it was a paid trip.

Check out: www.travelwriters.com.

When you have your own business as a creative non-fiction writer (or any writer keep in mind), you can write-off your travel expenses on your taxes in a country like Canada as long as you make an effort to publish the story you produce.

Meaning, you can go on a trip, write about it and even if you don't get it published – but you try – this is tax-deductible. Check into the tax laws in your country to discover if you can benefit from this terrific Canadian law.

Back to the actual writing of the travel story I will attempt to address questions such as:

- When do you describe place?

and,

- When should you describe the experience (action)?

In terms of when you should describe place, with creative non-fiction writing you really need to go with what interests you. Most likely, if it interests you, it will interest the reader. If you find a place fascinating and certain things capture your attention – make sure you share this with your readers.

When should you describe the experience (action)? Go with the same gut instincts. Writing is a wonderful experience where you actually get the rare opportunity to fully perform from your head, heart and gut. This is about giving it your all. Sometimes it's hard all the time, and then you have nothing left for yourself. However, make sure if you're involved with a particular experience while you're traveling and it stirs you – you share this with your readers.

Conclusion

Travel writing is a wonderful way to share your experiences with a wider audience as you see the world. If you don't have the budget to travel, you can also experience travel writing through www.travelwriters.com, as well as contacting the embassy or consulate where you live for the places you most like to discover.

Remember, you want to make sure your narrative in a travel piece is not in a shopping list style. You don't want to write in such a way where you say: first we went here, then we went there, and then we went...this becomes boring to the reader. What makes you read a travel piece? I bet it's when the writer actually gives his/her solid opinion about a place or thing and helps you to experience what they're experiencing.

Don't be afraid to write about emotions, thoughts, and any observations that you think would help the reader to fully understand what it's like to be in Italy, Paris, Durban, Prague, Rio de Janeiro to name a few places. You want the reader to feel, think, smell, hear and taste what you have. Write from the gut.

MID-CHAPTER ASSIGNMENT 1.9

Spend a bit of money getting on a tour bus in your town or city – or use public transit. Spend a day discovering the landmarks, historical sites, interesting restaurants, art galleries and museums, etc. Enjoy yourself. Take careful notes or bring a recorder or both. Make sure you prepare a two page story of your day in your town and post it to your personal website.

Now, we'll move onto analysis and reviews.

Analysis and Reviews

There are all kinds of reviews that can be done: theatre, opera, dance and ballet, movies, video games, music, software programs, books and media in general. It's also possible to review anything that you feel needs to be reviewed.

With reviews, you want to make sure you answer all the main questions of journalism: What is being reviewed? Why is it important? Where is this subject you've chosen and where can readers get access to it to form their own opinions? Who is involved? When has the event taken place, where is the publication, when is the release, etc.? As well as how will this affect your readers?

After you've done all that, you want to give your opinion on the subject you're reviewing. Be honest – your dishonesty will not serve your audience. If you give them the aforementioned facts about the subject of your review, your analysis is something they can choose to agree or disagree.

Using the basic elements of story-telling which we will discuss in the next chapter, you can produce valuable work of creative non-fiction writing.

Here is a short book review from Canada's *Globe and Mail* of December 10, 2005:

The Grand Tour: A Traveler's Guide to the Solar System By William K. Hartmann and Ron Miller, Workman, 296 pages, $27.95
- This is the completely updated and revised third edition of a terrifically detailed guide to the solar system. The fascinating tour includes more than 160 new, digitally enhanced paintings, as well as photos, maps and illustrations. A must for astronomy buss, students and anyone else who simply wants to know more about our heavenly neighbours in outer space.

Here is short movie review from Canada's *Globe and Mail* of August 19, 2006:

The Devil Wears Prada ***
• But God is in the details and a lucky thing too. In this adaptation of Lauren Weisberger's roman à clef about her stint at Vogue, it's the details – an occasional line of dialogue that rises to the level of wit, a slight plot turn that undermines our conditioned expectations, and especially a divinely nuanced performance by Meryl Streep as the diva-devil – that saves the picture from itself, from the banality of such commonplace evils as a predictable story arc with a pat message. The redemption may not be celestial, but give thanks for small mercies – this is a breezy and enjoyable piece of pop entertainment. PG (June 30) – R.G.

Continue to read many reviews in newspapers and magazines for more examples. Hopefully, this gives you a sense of the potential of long and short reviews.

Here's another sample review from the *Handbook of Magazine Article Writing* edited by Michelle Ruberg:

Wordcraft: The Art of Turning Little Words Into Big Business by Alex Frankel (Crown).

There's no better example of language's power in the marketplace than the actual brand names that appear there: Verizon, Accenture, Pontiac Aztek, Viagra. It's clear that the right product names – no matter how manufactured-sounding or nonsensical – equal big money for business.

Alex Frankel's *Wordcraft: The Art of Turing Little Words Into Big Business* (Crown) offers a glimpse at the secretive world of professional namers – writers and marketers who invent the catchy product names that sometimes creep into the cultural lexicon.

How much work went into name Lunchables? What popular tech device went through such tentative incarnations as Banjo, GamePlan, Hula, and Sling? (Answer: BlackBerry). It's astounding to learn how much trouble large corporations will go to (and how much money they'll spend) to achieve the perfect brand name. The level of secrecy surrounding naming projects is also remarkable, as tare the author's skills at worming his way into them. *Wordcraft*, with its relevant observations about what happens when language, pup culture, and capitalism intersect, is excellent journalism. It also might be the first book about brand marketing that's actually fun to read.

Tips on How to Write a Review

The first and extremely important tip to writing a review – let's use the example of a book – is to actually read it! Sounds simple, but there are many people who write reviews of books, plays, movies, etc. they haven't even seen. I too have done this with a play which happened in Montreal but I didn't actually see it.

I did write the article based on press material and used quotes from other newspapers that I hope actually saw it. I also stated in the story I had not seen the play. This makes doing this style of review far more ethical because the reader can more clearly know where you're coming from.

Remember writing is a written dialogue with your readers. It is a form of broadcasting. The same way you would want to share your experience of a movie, a play, a book, a television show, etc. with your friends is the way you want to write the review.

It needs to have a beginning, middle and end (also known as BME) like many stories do. Usually reviews do not have an inverted pyramid format, especially when written for magazines. You don't want to give away too many details so your readers will not want to discover the media form for themselves. However, you want to caution them against some things and perhaps highly recommend others.

Understanding how to write a review is as simple as following the basic storytelling practices outlined in chapter two. That's coming up, but for now let's try an exercise that will probably help you to see how much basic storytelling is ingrained in you once we reach chapter two.

I wrote a review of Cecil Foster's *Island Wings* for a weekly entertainment magazine called *Hour* in Montreal, Canada. The first thing I did was read the book. The second thing I did was start the story by giving a general outline of what the book is about – nothing far different from the information you can find on the back of a book jacket. Then, I moved into my analysis – which was balanced. There were things I liked about the book and things I didn't.

There are reviews which "slam" things. Some people like this sort of review that would go as far as to call a piece of work "garbage." Well, that's their personality. What I'm trying to teach you here are the tenets of journalism which means you always have to keep your judgment fair and your mind open to any artistic piece which exists. Surely, your honesty is important in a review. However, you must remember that for every "crap" movie or book that may actually exist – there is at least one person out there who would like it. This is true, or it wouldn't be open to the marketplace. This is why you need to keep an open mind with reviews and make sure you try to see some of the positive elements of a form of media.

Below are some examples of both positive and negative phrases you can use with different types of reviews. These examples should get you thinking about how to incorporate the proper language to describe particular products.

FOOD REVIEWS: Food reviews can include following recipes to test their effectiveness.

An example of a positive phrase: "A culinary theatre". A negative phrase is "this is a place for the budget conscious eater, but at this "cheap eats" you pay for what you get.

BOOK REVIEWS: This involves reading a book and reviewing it.
An example of a positive phrase would be "this is a page-turner." An example of a negative phrase is "this book will surely put you to sleep."

RESTAURANT REVIEWS: Usually involves going to a restaurant and reviewing it on a star system. The more stars, usually out of five, the better the restaurant. You would review on everything from ambiance to service to the quality of the food.

An example of a positive phrase would be "the atmosphere of this restaurant makes you feel like you're eating in your dream dining room." An example of a negative phrase would be "if you have a lot of time to kill then you won't mind the slow service."

MOVIE REVIEWS: When you go to a movie, you would review it, similar to how you would a book.

An example of a positive phrase is "you'll be thinking of this movie all year." An example of a negative phrase is "it's not worth the nine dollars."

THEATRE REVIEWS: When seeing plays, you would review it similar to how you would a movie.

An example of a positive phrase would be "you're sure to be left standing at the end of this fantastic play." An example of a negative phrase is "try not to heckle the performers during the performance. You'll be tempted to."

TV SHOW REVIEWS: When watching a new television program, you would review it similar to how you would a play.

An example of a positive phrase would be "I anticipate you'll be watching this show for many seasons to come." An example of a negative phrase is "this show is what remote controls were made for."

Conclusion

Review and analysis writing is enjoyable because it allows you to review and reflect on an art form and share your opinions with others. Please, try not to forget the power you have as a writer and make every effort not to abuse it – this could come back to haunt you. Try to note the positive things in any given review, even if you don't like it. Alternatively, if you adore it – try to maintain a critical stance in your writing – not everyone will like what you like. Your job is to give your honest opinion in a balanced story.

MID-CHAPTER ASSIGNMENT 1.10

Using the tools listed above write a well worded, high impact review on a movie you have seen recently. Don't look at other reviews of the movie to help you write yours. Just use your own opinions and memory recall to remember the quality of the acting, the strength of the plot, the beauty (or lack of) in the cinematography and so on.

You're review should be less than 230 words. Completed assignments can be uploaded to your personal website.

Conclusion

During this ebook and the ebook of your lifetime, you will probably have the opportunity to write about many different areas of writing mentioned here and not mentioned. This is just to give you a taste of the opportunities of where you can go with creative non-fiction.

The focus of this ebook is a lot like hard-news journalism, but it's a new form of journalism which Robert S. Boynton coins in his book *The New New Journalism*. The lifestyle one can lead as a creative non-fiction writer will be discussed later.

For now, even if you are just brushing your skills, or completely new to all this – I have an assignment to make sure you're taking in all this information.

ASSIGNMENT 1.11 GRADED

Here it is laid out step-by-step:

- Take any one form of the creative non-fiction writing styles mentioned and write a one page (max) story or review from your existing skills
- Make sure you create a title or headline for your story or review – if stuck with one, read newspapers and magazines for ideas on style
- If you know of a form of writing you would really like to try – go ahead! This ebook is about freedom. Just post your work on your personal website.

Just to let you know how I will be reviewing your assignment if you send me the link:

- I'm looking to see what your skills are at this point so it gives me a sense of how much I will need to groom you throughout this ebook
- The mark you will receive will be a simple (low – needs improvement, medium – shows promise, high – this man or woman can be a star writer)
- Please don't take the marking system personally and that's something you will need to get used to with writing. It's simply to give me a sense of what level you're at, which I mentioned before.

With that – good luck on your first assignment to be reviewed!

CHAPTER 2

BASIC ELEMENTS OF STORY-TELLING

Hello and welcome to chapter two on basic elements of story-telling. Here I will explain three story-telling techniques in writing: BME, inverted pyramid and the circle. We'll also discuss the importance of focusing your story. Let's start with focus – it's very important.

Focus

It may be wise to diversify a business, but your writing needs to have focus.

When I worked at the Canadian Broadcasting Corporation (CBC), one of the many things I learned was the importance of focus.

Many times I was trained on were how to create strong focus statements that included the word "because." For example, if I were doing a story on the number of people who are self-employed, I might create a basic focus statement like this,

Focus statement: The number of self-employed people is on the rise because job security is scarce in this millennium.

The reason for this focus statement which is meant to be written before writing anything is to make sure you stay on track. This keeps your writing focused. A key thing that many professional writers do after writing the focus statement is to constantly refer back to it if they feel like they're getting lost in the story. Plus, it helps you as the new or established writer; remember why you are writing the piece in the first place.

One of the points of this ebook is you can't come up with a focus statement until you have your idea – that's to be explored in the next chapter. Let's continue with BME. But first, another assignment – what fun!

MID-CHAPTER ASSIGNMENT 2.1

Think of a story idea you have been burning to work on for quite awhile. It may be the story which prompted you to buy this ebook. Write a one sentence focus statement with the word "because" included. Post your focus statement to your personal website.

Beginning, Middle, End (BME)

There's a phrase in journalism called BME. This stands for beginning, middle and end. It's the basic way most of us tell stories. A story can go something like this:

Beginning: I was rushing around my house to feed my cat and find my car keys to get to work. When I couldn't find my keys, I decided to take the bus.

Middle: I ran to the bus, missing it by seconds because I don't know the schedule. Once I checked the schedule I realized one wasn't coming until another 30 minutes. I flagged a taxi, the fourth one finally stopped and I jumped in to get to work.

End: Once I arrived, I was 45 minutes late and it was my first day. I lost my job and $20 on the cab ride.

This basic story has a beginning, middle and an end. Each paragraph can be seen as each part of BME.

To understand this concept, imagine you're telling a story to a friend or family member. You probably use BME all the time. It still works in the same way as fiction stories as well as using BME with creative non-fiction stories. The beginning is meant to warm the reader to your story. The middle is basically the climax and the end draws everything to a conclusion. Your aim is to leave the reader satisfied.

Things to remember:

In story-telling you don't want to leave your reader confused. This is the number one rule. Following the structure of BME has many advantages – it gives a natural flow to your writing. This is an admirable quality to have in any piece of writing – flow.

Some things to look out for are making sure you have answered all questions raised by your story. There are always exceptions to the rules and if you're writing a real-life mystery you may want to leave it as such at the end. However, in most cases, readers want their questions about the story answered. Since you don't have the luxury of being able to talk to them face-to-face, and this about the luxury of communicating through the written word, make sure you are clear.

That's why many writers in newspapers and magazines will include their email addresses at the end of a story so they can be contacted. Make yourself accessible to your readers so you can engage with them. They may have tips or ideas on how you can improve your writing. They may also simply want to praise you for your work. Alternatively, they may want to lambaste you for something you've written. Whatever the reason, getting used to praise, criticism and everything in between is just part of the business of writing.

BME has many advantages for certain types of stories. It works well with personal essays, travel pieces and even memoirs. It's your vivid writing that will engage the reader and this discussion of basic elements of story-telling is just the beginning of helping you to structure your pieces.

Here's another example from *The Toronto Star*, July 27, 2006. The story is titled, "Yukon crash ends faith mission" by Nasreen Gulamhussein and Steve Rennie:

Beginning: It began two weeks ago as a Muslim community outreach mission. Several men crossed the country by van, visiting Muslims from Toronto to Inuvik, N.W.T. to see how they lived how they practiced Islam.

Middle: They were due back in early August, but a fatal car crash above the Arctic Circle took the lives of five of them – four from Toronto, one from Whitehorse in the Yukon.

Only one man, Zafar Malik of Toronto, survived the crash.

The others, Azmat Sheikh, 38, Naoman Sidat, 56, Mohammed Saeed Manjawala, 33, Mohammed Pathan, 65, and Whitehorse resident Khalid Malik were killed Monday when their red minivan went off the road as it rounded a gravel turn on the Dempster Highway in the Yukon, said RCMP Sgt. Dan Gaudet.

The van, which was traveling south from Inuvik, then plunged 12 metres down a steep embankment, he said.

Reached yesterday by the Star in his Inuvik hospital room, Zafar Malik said Sidat, the driver, lost control on the gravel.

"We tried to put brakes on it to make it slower, and it just slipped. It went out of control. It rolled, rolled, rolled and went down. The road was so bad."

Initial response came from the nearest RCMP detachment in Fort McPherson, about 160 km away, after another driver reported the accident.

End: When paramedics arrived at the scene, four of the men were already dead and two were hurt. One of the injured men died at the crash scene and Zafar Malik was airlifted to an Inuvik hospital, where he is recovering.

Although the story continues more at length, this gives you a strong example of the BME method. I've indicated throughout the story where the beginning, middle and end are.

Also keep in mind that in writing some longer pieces like this one, sometimes to keep a strong structure for the piece, there may be more than one BME structure throughout the story. A story will have more than one beginning, more than one middle and more than one ending.

MID-CHAPTER ASSIGNMENT 2.2

Write a one page story following the BME format. Make sure your story has an extremely strong beginning, a strong middle and an unforgettable ending. Think of the most fantastic true story you've told and write about that in the BME format. Post your assignment to your personal website.

Inverted Pyramid

Pick up any newspaper, some magazines or even take time to read online and you will definitely find the inverted pyramid format.

Visualize the pyramids of Egypt. If you could shrink them with a magic wand, convert them into a shape you can see on your computer screen or notebook and write within those lines – what would you story read like?

Well, it would be like the stories you see on the front page of newspapers. All the important information is packed into the first few paragraphs. The least important information is included near the end. In terms importance, it funnels down. A funnel is another way to see this format.

With the speed many people live their lives these days; the inverted pyramid method has advantages because people can read the information quickly. Rather than spending the time to read an entire story like they may do with the BME method, they can read a few paragraphs and still get the gist of the story.

Writing in the inverted pyramid format takes more organization than the BME method. You need to make sure you understand the essence of your story and be able to get to the nuts and bolts fast. In the first paragraph, you want to make sure you have included the information you need – plus don't forget focus.

The inverted pyramid method also needs a lead. Journalists know about leads well.

Leads are when you basically included the focus of your story, written in a way that doesn't sound like a focus statement (unless it's wonderfully written), in the first paragraph. It should answer the question – why should I care about this story? This is true of your focus statement as well.

The difference between a lead in traditional journalism and in creative non-fiction is that it wouldn't take on a "newsy" sound. You as the writer have more liberty to include powerful phrases, vivid vocabulary and luxurious language. At the same time you want to make sure your writing is easy to read and understand – I'll tell you why.

Most commercial published writing is written at a grade 8 reading level. The reason for this is because not everyone has a high school education, higher level education or access to the Internet and libraries where they can learn in non-traditional ways. If you want to be read, you want to make yourself understandable. Use the KISS principle – Keep it Simple Stupid.

To continue with the inverted pyramid structure – the rest of the story should still flow, making sure paragraphs follow logically, it's answering the necessary questions of the reader and remains educational, as well as entertaining.

With the inverted pyramid method, you may want to include background research near the end which is less important information for the reader to know. With this method, you are giving the reader the option to know the basics in the first few paragraphs, or more by reading the entire article.

Here's an example from the front page of July 27, 2006's Globe and Mail by Shawna Richer and Gloria Galloway:

Prime Minister Stephen Harper under attack by political opponents over his Middle East policy, said yesterday he will seek explanations from the United Nations and the Israeli government about the "terrible tragedy" that killed a Canadian peacekeeper in Lebanon.

Mr. Harper described as "troubling" events surrounding the Israeli attack that killed four peacekeepers, including Canadian Major Paeta Derek Hess-von Kruedener, who was serving with the United Nations Truce Supervision Organization. Canadian officials characterized the major as missing and presumed dead.

These two first paragraphs of the story include the lead and most of the story. Near the end, it reads like this:

The Prime Mister said it is premature to say whether a UN peacekeeping force should be dispatched to Lebanon. But he said he would prefer Canada keep its troops out of Lebanon because a ceasefire between Israel and the Lebanese militant group Hezbollah should be enforced by Middle East countries. The United States has proposed a NATO-led intervention force in southern Lebanon and wants the UN to sanction it as it did for coalition forces in Afghanistan.

"There is no consensus on any kind international force in Lebanon, either from the UN or NATO," Mr. Harper said.

"I've made clear our preference would be not to see Canadian or foreign troops involved, but obviously we're prepared to work with the international community on whatever plan a consensus develops on."

The less important and more detailed information was included at the end of the story. This is standard inverted pyramid format which you can find in almost newspapers all over the world. Just reading the first paragraph or two usually gives 90 per cent of the information on what the article is about.

MID-CHAPTER ASSIGNMENT 2.3

Find examples of the inverted pyramid style you admire in your local newspaper and post a link to it on your personal website.

Circle

The circle method of writing is something I was taught by a terrific teaching assistant I had while I was at Carleton University in Ottawa, Canada.

I wrote an essay I thought was brilliant when I finished it, but it needed a lot of work with 20/20 hindsight. She helped tremendously by teaching me the circle method. (Notice I just told a story using the BME method).

The circle method is simple. It's based on the concept that life is a circle. All humans and living things come into this life as babies – needing care. Then, we grow up and we can be independent. Then we die – not to be morbid, but this is one of the sure things of life.

Writing is like capturing a slice of life, some stories; features in particular are referred to as "slice of life" pieces by editors at publications. The way you write the circle is by ending the story the way you begin.

Although I have said this style of writing is simple, some writers find it difficult – to others it comes naturally. It's a matter of truly understanding the beginning of your story. Rather than having an ending that doesn't connect to the beginning, such as in the BME method – you make sure your ending ties everything together with the beginning. You may even re-use words from the beginning paragraph.

Here's an example from one of my creative non-fiction stories.

Matoke

In the early 1980s, when I was 10 years old, things changed at my school with the arrival of a new vice-principal. At O'Connor Public School in Toronto, Canada, Mr. Goldberg set up a close-circuit television studio. The show the students and Mr. Goldberg produced was called OCTV News.

In a small room of the school that used to be the teachers' lounge, coffee makers and plastic cushions were replaced by an anchor's desk and a camera as big as me. A few grade 5 students, myself included, rotated through the various production jobs. Sometimes I was the sound engineer, which meant putting the needle on the Beatles song, "Here Comes the Sun", and our theme music. Sometimes I was the announcer, which meant telling Angelikki to show up to the Peter Pan play rehearsals. She was playing Peter, and I was Wendy.

One "International Day," we had to bring a dish from our heritage to be sampled by other students. Mr. Goldberg forgot it was International Day and did not write anything into our scripts about it for the OCTV News. That day I was co-announcing.

"Donna and Eric, just ad lib about the International Day after the news," said Mr. Goldberg seconds before we went on-air.

After the news, Eric asked me what dish I had brought in and I told him "matoke" - a common Ugandan meal made of steamed and mashed green bananas.

"Where is Uganda?" asked Eric.

"In Africa," I replied.

"Oh Africa! I thought they ate people there, I didn't know they ate food!" said Eric, and I almost burst into tears.

"I think there's a lot you don't know about Africa, Eric. My uncles, aunts and cousins who still live there do not eat people," I said, still forcing back the tears.

"Well what is Africa like?" he asked.

I had only been to Uganda as a baby; I was born and raised in Canada. My father came to Canada on a Commonwealth scholarship. When he returned to Uganda for a new job with a new wife and baby (that was me), Dictator Idi Amin was in power. We all escaped the country with only our lives.

I told Eric - and also about 500 other students who were watching OCTV - everything I knew about Uganda. I told them stories about my family who lived in a brick house, not a grass hut; who drove cars, not camels, and who ate matoke, rather than people. The response was phenomenal. Scores of students wanted to know more. They had questions, many of which I could not answer. I asked my teacher if my father could come to class and talk about Uganda. Soon afterwards, Daddy was standing at the front of the class with my globe piggy bank, rattling change as he turned it to point out Uganda.

My father said we fed those students with knowledge of African people. I guess we did feed those kids at O'Connor a lot more than matoke.
END

Another example of this style is the movie "Groundhog Day." The way this move begins is the same way it ends.

MID-CHAPTER ASSIGNMENT

Find examples of the circle method in a form of writing and post a link to it on your personal website.

Conclusion

Remember that with all the methods mentioned, focus is the first and most important thing as a start. Without it, your piece will be "all over the place." Readers don't have the time to figure out what you're trying to say.

It's like being a filmmaker – most moviegoers make up their mind about a film within the first few minutes. The difference is many of them won't ask for their money back once they're in the film and feeling completely bored.

With writing, they'll stop reading – you've just lost someone to communicate with, to deliver your message.

The three different story-telling styles we have discussed are BME, inverted pyramid and the circle.

BME, standing for beginning, middle and end, is similar to how you would tell a story to anyone you know. Inverted pyramid is a different style commonly found on the front page of newspapers and online. The circle is similar to the "circle of life" and the beginning mirrors the ending so everything comes around again.

ASSIGNMENT:

For the three methods we've discussed; BME, inverted pyramid and the circle choose one of the styles and post it to your personal website.

I will not be marking this assignment, but I will be reviewing it and so will your peers. Sharing your work with others is also known as peer review, or peer editing. It always helps to get another "set of eyes" looking at your stuff. This helps to make it great. Get in the habit of exposing your talents in writing to others. As readers and perhaps writers themselves, their opinion counts. Doesn't mean you need to listen – but, feedback always helps.

CHAPTER 3

STORY IDEAS AND RESEARCH METHODS

Hello and welcome to chapter three on story ideas and research methods. I'm sure many of you have a knack for writing or I sincerely hope you are finding this a help. Now, let's get down to digging for terrific story ideas and making them come alive with dynamic research.

Having a good idea is one of the most important starts to writing. Research is one of the most important parts to writing a good story. The word also means many things in creative non-fiction:

- Keeping track of ideas and finding them
- Library Research and Internet Research
- Gathering Research
- Finding Sources

Let's start with how to find story ideas.

Story Ideas

You may be the type of person that is already brimming with many ideas and that's why you're taking this ebook. Perhaps there's one burning idea you've been waiting to develop and that's the reason.

Whatever your reason, you must have ideas to write. Even keeping a shopping list is an idea and when using creative non-fiction, can turn into an extremely interesting topic.

I was discussing how people find ideas when we first worked on this ebook. Throughout my career in teaching, finding ideas is one of the common threads of discussion in journalism schools. Throughout my professional communications career, executives and journalists will spend hours in meetings at times – just discussing ideas for stories.

Ideas are an extremely important thing. Many working environments where writing is needed also must have a diverse group of people so the ideas become diverse. The exception to this is if it's a community newspaper pertaining to one group of people – or a magazine focused on single mothers. In the latter case, it may help to have many single mothers working at the magazine.

Whatever the publication or opportunity to get your creative non-fiction published, creating ideas is essential.

When a friend and I were discussing how people find ideas, we mentioned how important it is to draw from every aspect of your everyday life. People (and writers especially) are inspired by everything happening around them. Well, perhaps not everything – but, if something peaks your interest – go for it!

In journalism schools all over the world it's a hub of ideas. Students like you get their first chance of working in a "think tank" of ideas. Ideas are questioned and challenged, argued and approved, discussed and debated. You will have the opportunity to create this atmosphere online, with the prejudice line broken. You won't be able to see the face of the person talking to you – to be persuaded by beauty or what you perceive as lack t. It's a true democracy where people can voice their opinions and get feedback – as long as you can type, can afford an Internet connection, or have access to a computer.

In the professional writing world, some publications and news agencies pay top dollar for people to conduct focus groups and editorial boards just to diversify their contacts and create story ideas.

While I was working for the CBC back in 1995, I was a Diversity Journalist – one of my duties was creating editorial boards to discuss news coverage and forgotten story ideas, as well as expand their contact base.

You can hold your own focus groups among friends if you feel stumped for ideas. This can be formal or informal. You can throw an "idea party" where everyone there must come with one idea they haven't seen covered often, if at all in writing. While you're sitting around with friends and family, pay attention to the things they say, the things they're concerned about. Being a good listener will make it easier to be a good creative non-fiction writer.

There are so many ideas you can come up with just by listening to others.

As well, don't forget that many journalists get their ideas by paying attention to radio, TV, movies, the Internet, books, video games, newspapers and magazines to name a few. The media can inspire you to produce more media.

Ben Yagoda in the *Handbook of Magazine Article Writing* mentions that many writers get their ideas while in the shower. I take showers, but I also get many ideas while taking quick breaks from work. I get ideas while eating, while walking, while on the bus or driving. This goes back to what my colleague and I were talking about – you can draw ideas from every part of your everyday life.

Here are some solicited words of advice for keeping track of ideas:

- Keep a small notebook to write down ideas
- When you have an idea, write it down if you think it's important
- Depending on how comfortable you feel, share your ideas with others – even if someone else steals it, they won't write it exactly like you would unless they've plagiarized (we'll get into ethics later)
- With the before mentioned, remember there are some ideas that are so fresh and new – you should keep them to yourself and only share them with people you trust

Keep in mind the ideas you will be sharing with me in this ebook are yours – not mine. It would be unethical of me to steal any of your stories. This would simply make me look bad. I have a business and don't want that.

We'll get into ethics more later, but many people in the publishing industry are honest contrary to popular belief. Yes, there are always a few bad apples in the bunch. However, because being a successful writer of any genre, including creative non-fiction is based so much on reputation and spending a lifetime building one – in general, people don't stab others in the back. Keep this in mind and keep paranoia down.

Wow....that was a lot to say about story ideas. The crazy thing is there's more to say too. This subject could last for days, but let's move onto library research. As well, that's another thing to mention about how to get ideas – sometimes just browsing around a library can create loads of ideas – it's called serendipity.

Library and Internet Research

Libraries and librarians can be your best friends as a creative non-fiction writer. It's good to develop the skills of library research yourself, but librarians can really help when you're stuck. As well as being trained and educated professionals, they're also usually great at customer service. They love books and media as much as you do. That's how they make their living.

Again at the CBC, I actually worked for awhile as a Media Librarian in what is known as Visual Resources. This was a library where all visual media was kept and was used by journalists, producers, writers, researchers and editorial assistants. It was basically an archive of stock tape of CBC broadcasts.

As you may have noticed what I have done throughout this chapter with me, I've made reference to books that you might be able to find in your local library or on the Internet. I highly encourage you to read all books and Internet references mentioned, as well as to refer to the bibliography that will be included at the end of this ebook.

Speaking of books, there's a great one filled with many listings called *The Internet Handbook for Writers, Researchers and Journalists* by Mary McGuire, Linda Stilborne, Melinda McAdams and Laurel Hyatt. This book includes many links to resources you can use on the Internet to find out background material to your story ideas.

Also, libraries are the places where you can find the huge dictionaries you may not be able to afford or the *Farmer's Almanac* to create story ideas on upcoming events like anniversaries.

In most libraries around the world, there are also computers where you can use the Internet. You may be at one of them now learning this chapter. Most of these computers, such as the ones in Canadian libraries, allow you to access the local and national databases of resources. Also there are links to resources where you can access resources all over the world and suggestions for finding ideas:

- www.nytimes.com/learning - offers an "On This Day in History" archive that is great for doing stories on anniversaries.
- There's also *The Optimist's Guide to History* and *Pro Football Chronicle* that give you information on important dates in history for stories
- To get out of a writing rut, try reading things you don't usually read, like *Aeronautics Monthly* or *Modern Ferret*
- Shake up your life to come up with interesting stories
- Take a vacation or a break
- When finding sources, good places to start – ProfNet (www.profnet.com), sponsored by PR newswire
- Again, when finding sources, ExpertSource (www.bsuinesswire.com), backed by Business Wire
- Ask other writers – you can connect to other writers through I, the American Society of Journalists and Authors, the Periodical Writers Association of Canada, etc.
- Use professionals for expert advice, there is probably an *Encyclopedia of Associations* at your local library
- Public Relations people or PR people can be your friends for stories. Places like the University of Southern California have databases of experts: (http://uscnews.usc.edu/experts/index.html)
- Guestfinder (www.guestfinder.com) can put you in the direction of people who are experts
- Go through your own contacts

Simple ways of doing research include using popular search engines like Google.com and Yahoo.com. These search engines will give you access to many books.

The Internet itself has many resources that can be helpful. However, keep in mind just like with books – you must use the information with caution. It is sometimes said few people are more cynical than writers – this is not true for all, however, if you possess this quality, use it to your advantage. There are many ways to check if information you receive is valid. Always get at least a second opinion if you can, unless you're sure the first opinion is accurate. Go with your heart, gut and head when finding information – you're credibility as a creative non-fiction writer counts on it.

Gathering Research

Gathering information is a difficult task and sometimes becomes a burden. For some writers, this is the best part of writing, for others – they can't stand it. I recommend reading *The New New Journalism* book I mentioned before to find out how many writers of creative non-fiction handle research, but I will go into some points here.

With creative non-fiction, as also mentioned in *Writing Creative Fiction*, it can take days, weeks, months, even years to research a story. Think of Julia Roberts in the movie Erin Brokavich which won an Oscar for best actor. If you haven't seen the movie, she spent years investigating an environmental scandal that resulted in a law suit.

There are stories you will do creatively that will take you anywhere from minutes (depending on how fast you type)…..to years. It depends on what your interests are and how complicated the story. Something like a memoir for example is something you may be 40 years old and still writing, expecting to publish in another 40 years. Patience is an important thing to have with writing.

However, you may be working for a literary magazine where stories are produced month by month. You may also be working for a newspaper's Lifestyles section where stories are produced on a daily basis. You may also have your own website with advertising and earning a comfortable living and writing all day long as many stories as you can churn. As you can see, the situations vary.

Tom Wolfe, a pioneer in creative non-fiction, also known as the New Journalism, once said that you practically have to sleep with your subjects to really get to know them. Literally, this need not be true, however, this does raise an important point that Dan Wakefield mentions in his 1966 book called *Between the Lines* about the new journalism:

I am writing now for those readers – including myself – who have grown increasingly mistrustful of and bored with anonymous reports about the world, whether signed or unsigned, for those who have begun to suspect what we reporters of current events and problems so often try to conceal: that we are really individuals after all, not all-knowing, all-seeing Eyes but separate, complex, limited, particular "I"s.

With traditional journalism, many times a reader can sense the complete detachment involved in the reporting. Why so many readers love creative non-fiction and why so many writers love doing it is because it creates connections in this world where six degrees of separation means a lot. The more we know about a person, the better we can connect to them and the message they're trying to get across.

So, you don't need to get into bed with your sources, but you do need to understand them....to just about get to the point where you can read their minds. You'll see more why this is important when we get into internal and external dialogues in chapter five.

Finding Sources

Your research should help you to find sources. Through Internet searches, looking for people in the library, the person you talk to at the hot dog stand, your dentist, the sales associate you bought your shoes from – all these people are potential sources.

With the style of story for your writing, such as a memoir or personal piece, you may not have to go far or search wide for your sources.

An important tip that an extremely kind man told me at the Innoversity Creative Summit in Toronto, Canada (Innoversity being another word for diversity), was to keep a contact list.

We all have contacts – some of us may have the Queen of England on our list, some of us may have the butcher's name down the street. Depending on the story, all contacts are equally important. I recommend using a spreadsheet or finding special database software to keep your contacts handy.

Make sure as you keep this list, you also keeps notes about this person so you can remember them. Keep in mind this contact list could become public so use discretion when taking your notes about someone.

Finding sources is also about networking. Networking, or also simply put, getting to know as many people as you can, is important as a writer. Although writing can be a solitary service, you still need to take some time out of your schedule getting to know people. We'll expand on how to organize your time as a writer in chapter eight.

Conclusion

Finding story ideas can be one of the most exciting aspects of creative non-fiction writing. You can find them anywhere, and as mentioned above they are the main ingredient in cooking your stories.

Research can be done in a variety of ways. The most popular ways among many writers is using libraries and the Internet – all which can be found at your local library – or you may even want to draw from the library of books you have at home. If you're researching something which can become the type of story you would like to expand into a book – you might want to own the book and there are many second-hand bookstores, independent bookstores and places like Indigo, Chapters and Amazon.com which can supply you with what you need. When we get to the business part of writing in chapter 11, we'll talk about how you can make writing your business and write off many of your expenses with your taxes.

Finding sources and keeping a contact list is something that will help you move from a good writer to a terrific writer. Use a software package to create your contact list. Many PC computers have Microsoft database software which is a program I've used and find helpful. Whatever you choose to use, especially if you're a MAC or Linux user, the important thing is to make sure you keep track of your contacts because sometimes when faced with blocks for ideas – all you need to do is browse over your contact list for brilliant ideas to come.

ASSIGNMENT:

Come up with the story idea you would like to do for the final assignment in this ebook. Refer back to the first chapter for mention of the final assignment. To refresh your memory, it is a story of no more than 10 pages based on the different story styles explained in chapter one.

Next, develop a backgrounder for your story idea. A backgrounder is like developing a bibliography of sources, books, songs, newspaper and magazine articles, etc. that will aid in developing your story idea.

The backgrounder should contain the following:

- One half-page outlining your story idea
- Pages including your sources list
- Plus, a bibliography

After you've done this, post your backgrounder on your personal website and I will be marking it with the same criteria as chapter one's major assignment if you send me the link.

CHAPTER 4

CREATIVE NON-FICTION ETHICS, LEGAL ISSUES AND OTHER IMPORTANT STUFF

Hello and welcome to chapter four on creative non-fiction ethics, legal issue and other important stuff. The last part may seem vague, but just hang in there and you'll be pleasantly surprised.

This is that black and white area where if you choose to only keep your lies "white," then you will be in the black. I've used two books as a guide in explaining this to you.

The first is *Writing Creative Nonfiction* by Theodore A. Rees Cheney. Some of the important things to keep in mind:

- Diction
- Irony and humour
- Internal monologues
- Expanding on the truth
- Plain style
- Legal stuff
- Fictional bits

Diction

We haven't yet discussed the use of dialogue in a piece – but when trying to capture the essence of a person's speech there are some things to keep in mind.

It is your obligation as a writer to truly capture the way the person talks as a writer. Everyone has an accent – everyone. Meaning, everyone has a way of speaking that is different from someone else. It is up to you to listen carefully to the way a person expresses themselves and make sure you take careful notes.

This is important because each person is different and you can easily distinguish between a volley of dialogue in a piece by distinguishing between the uniqueness of the way people talk. The gurgles of a baby, although their language is not documented in the Oxford dictionary can still add a deep richness to your writing.

If the person is grammatically incorrect – quote them. If they are politically incorrect, quote them. If they use profanity...we'll discuss this next.

Just like when you're watching TV and you see the notice come on the screen that this program may be more suitable for mature audiences – you want to use this style when you're dealing with your editors.

Flag to them (flag meaning take notice in this case, rather than follow-up); the fact the piece contains profanity.

A note to the wise – know your audience. If you're writing for a children's magazine, it's obviously not wise to use profanity.

Here's an example of the complexity of diction and language usage from the preface of *The Canadian Reporter: News Writing and Reporting* by Catherine McKercher and Carman Cumming:

A Note on Pronouns

While reading this text you'll note that the authors have wrestled with one of the most common problems facing English-language writers, the lack of a neutral third-person pronoun.

In the past, common practice was to use "he" as the generic pronoun. Though grammatically acceptable, this practice is troubling because it tends to make women readers feel excluded.

Some modern authors deal wit the problem by rewording to avoid the singular pronoun or by avoiding pronouns altogether. This works well in some cases, but in others it sacrifices clarity. For that reason we have chosen, in cases where a singular pronouns is desirable, to vary the gender – using "he" in roughly half the examples and "she" in the rest.

We feel this approach works well. We hope you agree.

The Elements of Style by William Strunk Jr. and E.B. White is an excellent resource for punctuation and grammar. Here is a quick refresher:

Nouns: according to the Gage Canadian dictionary, a noun is a person, a place or a thing. They also note it's a quality, an event, etc.

Examples: person – Donna K (Me), place – United States, thing – shoes, event – World AIDS conference

Pronouns: again, according to the Gage Canadian dictionary – a pronoun is a word used instead of a noun.

Examples: he, she, it, that

Verbs: expresses an action.

Examples: fight, struggle, sing, dance, play, listen, and hear

Adjectives: used to describe a noun.

Examples: beautiful, wonderful, rainy, sunny, snowy, tropical, dry

Irony and Humour

Words can heal…words can hurt – remember that and it will make you a better writer.

In term of ethics, using words that heal is highly ethical. In terms of ethics, using words that hurt is not.

Keeping in mind what I said before about diction – if a source says something that may truly be funny, but would hurt even one person's feelings – that's a reader you may have lost. It's simply not good business. Of all the books in this world, you can only please some of the people some of the time. As a writer and if you want to make this your livelihood in a mainstream or "lefty" alternative fashion – which most creative non-fiction writers generally fall into – watch your mouth, your pen, your typing and your thoughts.

Here is an example of some irony and humour from *The National Post*'s columnist Shinan Govani, dated August 10, 2006:

You never do know who's going to show up at the bar on the top of the Park Hyatt.

One day it's Jude Law and his main-est squeeze; the next, it's a certain Alfie from Parliament Hill.

Not long ago, a source informs, that movie star couple – Jude and Sienna Miller – held court on the vertigo-chic terrace of the hotel bar. She then went to a semi-private audience with the Law. (She spent a good deal of her time on Jude's lap, is what I mean to say.)

"She was on him like a kid," is how one person describes the terribly droll vignette.

If only he'd had a sucker for her, the scene would have been complete. But, sadly, he didn't and the poor girl had to settle for just the lap – and a view, we suppose, of the Royal Ontario Museum.

I hope you find this as amusing as I do. There are a few turns of phrases here and the entire situation is drôle – "funny" in French.

The English language is a strange one and was built in an oppressive situation historically. However, I've just delivered the bad news – the good news is that words like "fantastic" make me smile just by writing them. When I hear them they sound even more beautiful. We'll get into word-use more in chapter five and six.

Here's an example from *The Art and Craft of Feature Writing* by William E. Blundell about infusing humour in a story. Blundell uses an example from Marilyn Chase about a different park in San Francisco. The story was printed in 1981:

San Francisco has long been toasted as one of the world's easiest places to get drunk and stay drunk. It has the requisite amenities: relatively cheap liquor, a temperate climate, and legions of tourists who are easy marks for a practiced panhandler. Now, to these attractions is added another: a park dedicated exclusively to winos....

Wino Park, officially called Sixth Street Park, is a transformed sandlot tucked amid the transient hotels, pawn shops and liquor stores of the city's tough South-of-Market area. There, a wino can recline with a bottle of Thunderbird or Night Train Express wine, build a bonfire, cook a meal, sleep, loiter or play a game of sodden volleyball without being arrested. A brass plaque commemorates famous people like a roll call of heroes: "Honoring: Winston Churchill, Ernest Hemingway, W. E. Fields, John Barrymore, Betty Ford, Janis Joplin, Dylan Thomas.....," they intone....

On a mild and sunny afternoon, they are among the tree dozen regulars who congregate in the tiny park. To an outsider, the first sensations suggest that this is some kind of crazy, landlocked beach party: blowing sand from the arid planters, the smell of woodsmoke from a midday bonfire, outdoor cooking, the blare of a radio tuned to soul and gospel music, and people drinking from Styrofoam cups.

A.W., 60 and gray-bearded, is the park's elder statesman. He occupies a chair next to the bonfire and despite the balmy spring day wear a fake Persian-lamb hat. It is adorned with a button that reads, "I'm alive," the slogan of Glide Memorial Church. "Winter was rough," he says slowly, "but it's alright now. All right." Hogshead, glowering and blind drunk, sits alone in a corner. He is the park's wood gatherer.

Ben, about 50, assumed the leadership role from S.Q. He is a robust black man with salt-and-pepper hair, print polyester shirt and a vest with a nametag reading "Glide staff. My name is Ben." He surveys the park with a proprietary eye and says the winos are holding their ground in perpetual turf battles with drug traffickers.

"I be here every day, seven days a week, from 6:30 in the morning. If I pick up a broom, everybody here will do the same," he says with an expansive gesture.

Ben's steady lady is Peggy, 34, a plump, freckled, toothless, ponytailed bacchante attired in fuzzy slippers and a shapeless plaid shirt. Her conversation indicates that somewhere, there lurks a proper, middle-class upbringing. She asks a reporter for a stock tip, and when none is forthcoming, explains: "My broker is in Connecticut, and anyway, I don't trust him. But if I were investing, I'd buy Kimberly-Clark, because of the Rely tampon scandal....."

Using a wealth of vocabulary, Chase was able to discuss the poverty among the people in Wino Park and bring them to life. I find her most brilliant point of humour is when Peggy asks her for the stock tips and talks about her broker being in Connecticut. However, there are many elements to find amusing in this story about a serious topic which turns it into a slice-of-life piece.

Also note that by the end of this ebook you'll have learnt how to create pieces like this which use research to start your story, narration to tell your story and dialogue to bring your story to life.

Internal Monologues

Again, we haven't discussed dialogue yet – that's coming in chapter six and there will be an assignment with that chapter.

Just to explain a little now....when I was talking about research earlier, sometimes you can get so close to your subjects with creative non-fiction writing you either are or feel like you're sleeping with them.

This gives many writers the freedom to feel they can write "internal monologues," or feel like they are reading a person's mind. An example can be when you're chatting with one of your family members and you mention a friend of yours they know. When you're speaking with your friend, you may mention that your mother or father says "hello," even if they didn't actually say that. You just know they would – kind of like you read their mind or know them well enough to know they would say that.

Whether you believe in mind-reading or not – Tom Wolfe and Gay Talese are some of the most common users of this style. Keep in mind it's hotly debated and many people, including many traditional journalists who have been in the business twice my lifetime don't agree with this style.

With this in mind....you can decide for you. I will explain the style and hopefully you will show the initiative to practice it. Read Wolfe, Talese and Capote and you will probably get a good sense of how you think it works. If you find it fits your style, go for it. If you like debating, you can always go on the online forums to defend your point for using the method or not.

Expanding on the truth

True non-fiction writing must be the truth, the whole truth and nothing but the truth – no buts about it.

If you are weaving pieces of information from various sources, some of it being it true and some t being false – this is not creative non-fiction – it's fiction. Non-fiction is based on facts. The creative element comes with your vivid vocabulary, dynamic dialogue, rich research, etc. I hope this is enough said.

Plain Style

Cheney in her book *Writing Creative Nonfiction* expresses concern that she may be encouraging non-fiction writers to write non-factual information. To be honest, when I saw this book (although it looked interesting); I was concerned about the same thing.

Although your writing should be creative, your facts must be accurate. Creative non-fiction is based on gathering facts. A good example of understanding this kind of journalism is reading Truman Capote's *In Cold Blood*. This is probably one of the best creative non-fiction, new journalism, new new journalism – whatever anyone wants to call it – it's all the same thing. It's a superb book – make sure you read it if you haven't already. Or, you could always see the movie in DVD.

Legal Stuff

While doing extra research for this ebook (I've been researching this ebook the majority of my life through my writing, educational and professional experience), I felt passionate about re-reading *The Canadian Press Stylebook*. Centennial College where I teach uses this guide for its print-based books.

Since all writers worldwide don't have access to this information unless you visit The Canadian Press's (CP's) website and order, I will make it simple by expressing just a bit of what it says from page 101, and see this as Journalism Ethics 101:

1. Carelessness and bad judgment on legal questions can ruin people's live. Every journalist must weigh this responsibility when working.
2. It is dangerous to publish statements that damage a person's reputation or livelihood unless the statements are provably true or unless the law clearly provides a special exemption.
3. It is particularly dangerous to suggest criminal conduct unless it has been proved in the courts.
4. Every person charged and before the courts is entitled to be presumed innocent and to receive a fair trial. It is forbidden to publish anything that passes judgment on an accused or that could hinder a fair trial unless it has been admitted in court as evidence. (Of course, the court's judgment is publishable).
5. Juveniles involved with the law – accused, witnesses or victims – must not be identified, even indirectly, without legal advice.
6. In cases where legal action is a possibility, or could involve a dispute over what was said, reporters should keep notes, audio tapes and related documents for three months. It's expected that notification of any legal action would be given by that time. Reporters should also note that during examination for discovery related to the story in question – including such things as e-mails to sources or other versions of the story.

These rules are based on Canadian law and it's different in different countries. However, keeping some of these things in mind will help you with legal issues. Some other important things to remember, on page 102 of CP's stylebook

1. Check legal authority before writing anything legally doubtful.
2. Cut out anything that looks legally questionable until it can be cleared for use.
3. If legal doubts arise after a story has been distributed, order the story killed or withheld immediately until the doubts can be resolved.

Conclusion

As you can see there is a lot to keep in mind when it comes to ethics and legal stuff. Discussing copyright and the legal elements of running your own business as a writer will be discussed in chapter 11.

Logical Fallacies

Logical fallacies: This phrase represents the content which is often used in media that presents information that can be misleading to the reader.

What is normally done in the opinion and editorials, as well as in some general articles found in newspapers, magazines and online are argumentative type of stories. With the foundation of a "slant," meaning the angle of the story – the writer is supporting the focus of their story by presenting the facts. This produces a story which may be representative of truth in society – as well as being viewed as a sound argument.

A logical fallacy on the other hand is an error in reasoning. The facts are presented, or what is perceived as the facts, but they may actually not lead to a conclusion of truth.

Here are some examples of logical fallacies.

1. Inductive Argument

Premise 1: Most American cats are domestic house cats.
Premise 2: Bill is an American cat.
Conclusion: Bill is domestic house cat.

This is a fallacy because the conclusion does not take into consideration the margin of error in premise one.

2. Factual Error

Columbus is the capital of the United States.

This is a fallacy because Washington, not Columbus is the capital of the United States. It's completely untrue.

3. Deductive Fallacy

Premise 1: If Portland is the capital of Maine, then it is in Maine.
Premise 2: Portland is in Maine.
Conclusion: Portland is the capital of Maine.
(Portland is in Maine, but Augusta is the capital.)

This is a fallacy because it runs along the same belief that because both Toronto and Ottawa are in Ontario, that would make Toronto the capital of Canada. This is also untrue along with the above. Actually, Ottawa is the capital of Canada.

4. Inductive Fallacy

Premise 1: Having just arrived in Ohio, I saw a white squirrel.
Conclusion: All Ohio Squirrels are white.
(While there are many, many squirrels in Ohio, the white ones are very rare).

This is a fallacy because it's based on assumptions.

The following are also fallacies:

- Ad Hominem – from Latin to English, "Ad Hominem" means "against the man" or "against the person." It takes this form:

1. Person A makes claim X.
2. Person B makes an attack on person A.
3. Therefore A's claim is false.

It is a fallacy because usually the claim or the attack is not the truth. An example:

1. Bill: "I believe that abortion is morally wrong."
   Dave: "Of course you would say that, you're a priest."
   Bill: "What about the arguments I gave to support my position?"
   Dave: "Those don't count. Like I said, you're a priest, so you have to say that abortion is wrong. Further, you are just a lackey to the Pope, so I can't believe what you say."

- Appeal to Authority – this fallacy is committed when a person is not a legitimate authority on the subject. More formally, if person A is not qualified to make reliable claims in subject S, then the argument will be fallacious.

- Appeal to Emotion – the article above uses this technique. This fallacy is committed when someone manipulates peoples' emotions in order to get them to accept a claim as being true. More formally, this sort of "reasoning" involves the substitution of various means of producing strong emotions in place of evidence for a claim. If the favorable emotions associated with X influence the person to accept X as true because they "feel good about X," then he has fallen prey to the fallacy.

- Appeal to Fear – the article above uses this technique.

More examples of the appeal to fear:

1. "You know, Professor Smith, I really need to get an A in this class. I'd like to stop by during your office hours later to discuss my grade. I'll be in your building anyways, visiting my father. He's your dean, by the way. I'll see you later."

2. "I don't think a Red Ryder BB rifle would make a good present for you. They are very dangerous and you'll put your eye out. Now, don't you agree that you should think of another gift idea?"

3. You must believe that God exists. After all, if you do not accept the existence of God, then you will face the horrors of hell."

4. "You shouldn't say such things against multiculturalism! If the chair heard what you were saying, you would never receive tenure. So, you had just better learn to accept that it is simply wrong to speak out against it."

- Appeal to Popularity – the Appeal to Popularity has the following form:

1. Most people approve of X (have favorable emotions towards X).
2. Therefore X is true.

The basic idea is that a claim is accepted as being true simply because most people are favorably inclined towards the claim. More formally, the fact that most people have favorable emotions associated with the claim is substituted in place of actual evidence for the claim. A person falls prey to this fallacy if he accepts a claim as being true simply because most other people approve of the claim.

Bandwagon – the Bandwagon is a fallacy in which a threat of rejection by one's peers (or peer pressure) is substituted for evidence in an "argument." This line of "reasoning" has the following form:

1. Person P is pressured by his/her peers or threatened with rejection.
2. Therefore person P's claim X is false.

This line of "reasoning" is fallacious because peer pressure and threat of rejection do not constitute evidence for rejecting a claim. This is especially clear in the following example:

Joe: "Bill, I know you think that 1+1=2. But we don't accept that sort of thing in our group."

Bill: "I was just joking. Of course I don't believe that."

It is clear that the pressure from Bill's group has no bearing on the truth of the claim that 1+1=2.

It should be noted that loyalty to a group and the need to belong can give people very strong reasons to conform to the views and positions of those groups. Further, from a practical standpoint we must often compromise our beliefs in order to belong to groups. However, this feeling of loyalty or the need to belong simply does not constitute evidence for a claim.

• Begging the Question – Begging the Question is a fallacy in which the premises include the claim that the conclusion is true or (directly or indirectly) assume that the conclusion is true. This sort of "reasoning" typically has the following form.

1. Premises in which the truth of the conclusion is claimed or the truth of the conclusion is assumed (either directly or indirectly).
2. Claim C (the conclusion) is true.

This sort of "reasoning" is fallacious because simply assuming that the conclusion is true (directly or indirectly) in the premises does not constitute evidence for that conclusion. Obviously, simply assuming a claim is true does not serve as evidence for that claim. This is especially clear in particularly blatant cases: "X is true. The evidence for this claim is that X is true."

Some cases of question begging are fairly blatant, while others can be extremely subtle.

Examples of Begging the Question

1. "If such actions were not illegal, then they would not be prohibited by the law."
2. "The belief in God is universal. After all, everyone believes in God."
3. Interviewer: "Your resume looks impressive but I need another reference." Bill: "Jill can give me a good reference."

Interviewer: "Good. But how do I know that Jill is trustworthy?"
Bill: "Certainly. I can vouch for her."

- Burden of Proof – Burden of Pros a fallacy in which the burden of pros placed on the wrong side. Another version occurs when a lack of evidence for side A is taken to be evidence for side B in cases in which the burden of proof actually rests on side B. A common name for this is an Appeal to Ignorance. This sort of reasoning typically has the following form:

1. Claim X is presented by side A and the burden of proof actually rests on side B.
2. Side B claims that X is false because there is no proof for X.

In many situations, one side has the burden of proof resting on it. This side is obligated to provide evidence for its position. The claim of the other side, the one that does not bear the burden of proof, is assumed to be true unless proven otherwise. The difficulty in such cases is determining which side, if any, the burden of proof rests on. In many cases, settling this issue can be a matter of significant debate. In some cases the burden of pros set by the situation. For example, in American law a person is assumed to be innocent until proven guilty (hence the burden of pros on the prosecution). As another example, in debate the burden of pros placed on the affirmative team. As a final example, in most cases the burden of proof rests on those who claim something exists (such as Bigfoot, psychic powers, universals, and sense data).

Examples of Burden of Proof

1. Bill: "I think that some people have psychic powers."
Jill: "What is your proof?"
Bill: "No one has been able to prove that people do not have psychic powers."

2. "You cannot prove that God does not exist, so He does."

- Confusing Cause and Effect – Confusing Cause and Effect is a fallacy that has the following general form:

1. A and B regularly occur together.
2. Therefore A is the cause of B.

This fallacy requires that there is not, in fact, a common cause that actually causes both A and B.

This fallacy is committed when a person assumes that one event must cause another just because the events occur together. More formally, this fallacy involves drawing the conclusion that A is the cause of B simply because A and B are in regular conjunction (and there is not a common cause that is actually the cause of A and B). The mistake being made is that the causal conclusion is being drawn without adequate justification.

In some cases it will be evident that the fallacy is being committed. For example, a person might claim that an illness was caused by a person getting a fever. In this case, it would be quite clear that the fever was caused by illness and not the other way around. In other cases, the fallacy is not always evident. One factor that makes causal reasoning quite difficult is that it is not always evident what the cause is and what is the effect. For example, a problem child might be the cause of the parents being short tempered or the short temper of the parents might be the cause of the child being problematic. The difficulty is increased by the fact that some situations might involve feedback. For example, the parents' temper might cause the child to become problematic and the child's behavior could worsen the parents' temper. In such cases it could be rather difficult to sort out what caused what in the first place.

In order to determine that the fallacy has been committed, it must be shown that the causal conclusion has not been adequately supported and that the person committing the fallacy has confused the actual cause with the effect. Showing that the fallacy has been committed will typically involve determining the actual cause and the actual effect. In some cases, as noted above, this can be quite easy. In other cases it will be difficult. In some cases, it might be almost impossible. Another thing that makes causal reasoning difficult is that people often have very different conceptions of cause and, in some cases; the issues are clouded by emotions and ideologies. For example, people often claim violence on TV and in movies must be censored because it causes people to like violence. Other people claim that there is violence on TV and in movies because people like violence. In this case, it is not obvious what the cause really is and the issue is clouded by the fact that emotions often run high on this issue.

While causal reasoning can be difficult, many errors can be avoided with due care and careful testing procedures. This is due to the fact that the fallacy arises because the conclusion is drawn without due care. One way to avoid the fallacy is to pay careful attention to the temporal sequence of events. Since (outside of Star Trek), effects do not generally precede their causes, if A occurs after B, then A cannot be the cause of B. However, these methods go beyond the scope of this program.

All causal fallacies involve an error in causal reasoning. However, this fallacy differs from the other causal fallacies in terms of the error in reasoning being made. In the case of a Post Hoc fallacy, the error is that a person is accepting that A is the cause of B simply because A occurs before B. In the case of the Fallacy ignoring a Common Cause A is taken to be the cause of B when there is, in fact, a third factor that is the cause of both A and B. For more information, see the relevant entries in this program.

Examples of Confusing Cause and Effect

1. It is claimed by some people that severe illness is caused by depression and anger. After all, people who are severely ill are very often depressed and angry. Thus, it follows that the cause of severe illness actually is the depression and anger. So, a good and cheerful attitude is key to staying healthy.

2. Bill sets out several plates with bread on them. After a couple days, he notices that the bread has mold growing all over it. Bill concludes that the mold was produced by the bread going bad. When Bill tells his mother about his experiment, she tells him that the mold was the cause of the bread going bad and that he better clean up the mess if he wants to get his allowance this week.

- Guilt by Association – the article above uses this technique – Guilt by Association is a fallacy in which a person rejects a claim simply because it is pointed out that people she dislikes accept the claim. This sort of "reasoning" has the following form:

1. It is pointed out that people person A does not like accept claim P.
2. Therefore P is false

It is clear that sort of "reasoning" is fallacious. For example the following is obviously a case of poor "reasoning": "You think that 1+1=2. But, Adolf Hitler, Charles Manson, Joseph Stalin, and Ted Bundy all believed that 1+1=2. So, you shouldn't believe it."

The fallacy draws its power from the fact that people do not like to be associated with people they dislike. Hence, if it is shown that a person shares a belief with people he dislikes he might be influenced into rejecting that belief. In such cases the person will be rejecting the claim based on how he thinks or feels about the people who hold it and because he does not want to be associated with such people.

Of course, the fact that someone does not want to be associated with people she dislikes does not justify the rejection of any claim. For example, most wicked and terrible people accept that the earth revolves around the sun and that lead is heavier than helium. No sane person would reject these claims simply because this would put them in the company of people they dislike (or even hate).

Example of Guilt by Association

1. Jen and Sandy are discussing the topic of welfare. Jen is fairly conservative politically but she has been an active opponent of racism. Sandy is extremely liberal politically.

Jen: "I was reading over some private studies of welfare and I think it would be better to have people work for their welfare. For example, people could pick up trash, put up signs, and maybe even do skilled labor that they are qualified for. This would probably make people feel better about them and it would get more out of our tax money."

Sandy: "I see. So, you want to have the poor people out on the streets picking up trash for their checks? Well, you know that is exactly the position David Count endorses."

Jen: "Who is he?"

Sandy: "I'm surprised you don't know him, seeing how alike you two are. He was a Grand Mooky Wizard for the Aryan Pure White League and is well known for his hatred of blacks and other minorities. With your views, you'd fit right in to his little racist club."

Jen: "So, I should reject my view just because I share it with some racist?"
Sandy: "Of course."

• Hasty Generalization – this fallacy is committed when a person draws a conclusion about a population based on a sample that is not large enough. It has the following form:

1. Sample S, which is too small, is taken from population P.
2. Conclusion C is drawn about Population P based on S.

The person committing the fallacy is misusing the following type of reasoning, which is known variously as Inductive Generalization, Generalization, and Statistical Generalization:

1. X% of all observed A's are B"s.
2. Therefore X% of all A's are Bs.

The fallacy is committed when not enough A's are observed to warrant the conclusion. If enough A's are observed then the reasoning is not fallacious.

Small samples will tend to be unrepresentative. As a blatant case, asking one person what she thinks about gun control would clearly not provide an adequate sized sample for determining what Canadians in general think about the issue. The general idea is that small samples are less likely to contain numbers proportional to the whole population. For example, if a bucket contains blue, red, green and orange marbles, then a sample of three marbles cannot possible be representative of the whole population of marbles. As the sample size of marbles increases the more likely it becomes that marbles of each color will be selected in proportion to their numbers in the whole population. The same holds true for things others than marbles, such as people and their political views.

Since Hasty Generalization is committed when the sample (the observed instances) is too small, it is important to have samples that are large enough when making a generalization. The most reliable way to do this is to take as large a sample as is practical. There are no fixed numbers as to what counts as being large enough. If the population in question is not very diverse (a population of cloned mice, for example) then a very small sample would suffice. If the population is very diverse (people, for example) then a fairly large sample would be needed. The size of the sample also depends on the size of the population. Obviously, a very small population will not support a huge sample. Finally, the required size will depend on the purpose of the sample. If Bill wants to know what Joe and Jane thinks about gun control, then a sample consisting of Bill and Jane would (obviously) be large enough. If Bill wants to know what most Australians think about gun control, then a sample consisting of Bill and Jane would be far too small.

People often commit Hasty Generalizations because of bias or prejudice. For example, someone who is a sexist might conclude that all women are unfit to fly jet fighters because one woman crashed one. People also commonly commit Hasty Generalizations because of laziness or sloppiness. It is very easy to simply leap to a conclusion and much harder to gather an adequate sample and draw a justified conclusion. Thus, avoiding this fallacy requires minimizing the influence of bias and taking care to select a sample that is large enough.

One final point: a Hasty Generalization, like any fallacy, might have a true conclusion. However, as long as the reasoning is fallacious there is no reason to accept the conclusion based on that reasoning.

Examples of Hasty Generalization

1. Smith, who is from England, decides to attend graduate school at Ohio State University. He has never been to the US before. The day after he arrives, he is walking back from an orientation session and sees two white (albino) squirrels chasing each other around a tree. In his next letter home, he tells his family that American squirrels are white.

2. Sam is riding her bike in her home town in Maine, minding her own business. A station wagon comes up behind her and the driver starts beeping his horn and then tries to force her off the road. As he goes by, the driver yells "get on

the sidewalk where you belong!" Sam sees that the car has Ohio plates and concludes that all Ohio drivers are jerks.

• Personal Attack – the article above uses this technique – a personal attack is committed when a person substitutes abusive remarks for evidence when attacking another person's claim or claims. This line of "reasoning" is fallacious because the attack is directed at the person making the claim and not the claim itself. The truth value of a claim is independent of the person making the claim. After all, no matter how repugnant an individual might be, he or she can still make true claims.

Not all ad Hominems are fallacious. In some cases, an individual's characteristics can have a bearing on the question of the veracity of her claims. For example, if someone is shown to be a pathological liar, then what he says can be considered to be unreliable. However, such attacks are weak, since even pathological liars might speak the truth on occasion.

In general, it is best to focus one's attention on the content of the claim and not on who made the claim. It is the content that determines the truth of the claim and not the characteristics of the person making the claim.

Examples of Personal Attack

1. In a school debate, Bill claims that the President's economic plan is unrealistic. His opponent, a professor, retorts by saying "the freshman has his facts wrong."
2. "This theory about a potential cure for cancer has been introduced by a doctor who is a known lesbian feminist. I don't see why we should extend an invitation for her to speak at the World Conference on Cancer."
3. "That claim cannot be true. Dave believes it, and we know how morally repulsive he is."
4. "Bill claims that Jane would be a good treasurer. However I find Bill's behavior offensive, so I'm not going to vote for Jill."
5. "Jane says that drug use is morally wrong, but she is just a goody-two shoes Christian, so we don't have to listen to her."

- Slippery Slope – the Slippery Slope is a fallacy in which a person asserts that some event must inevitably follow from another without any argument for the inevitability of the event in question. In most cases, there are a series of steps or gradations between one event and the one in question and no reason is given as to why the intervening steps or gradations will simply be bypassed. This "argument" has the following form:

1. Event X has occurred (or will or might occur).
2. Therefore event Y will inevitably happen.

This sort of "reasoning" is fallacious because there is no reason to believe that one event must inevitably follow from another without an argument for such a claim. This is especially clear in cases in which there are a significant number of steps or gradations between one event and another.

Examples of Slippery Slope

1. "We have to stop the tuition increase! The next thing you know, they'll be charging $40,000 a semester!"
2. "The US shouldn't get involved militarily in other countries. Once the government sends in a few troops, it will then send in thousands to die."
3. "You can never give anyone a break. If you do, they'll walk all over you."
4. "We've got to stop them from banning pornography. Once they start banning one form of literature, they will never stop. Next thing you know, they will be burning all the books!"

The above is just an example of some of the more common "logical fallacies" which can be found in media. The information is from The Nizkor Project which can also be found on the Internet for more information. They are presented to you in this chapter so you, as a budding writer, can avoid this type of sloppy journalism and communication and ensure you present sound arguments. Help to develop a generation of journalists that can all be respected for their honesty, bringing more honour to the profession.

Here's an article that is peppered with logical fallacies. When you read newspapers, even the most reputable of journalist are guilty confusing their writing with logical fallacies. They do this because it helps create an emotional story. This doesn't make it right, this makes it sell. There is a big difference. As a non-fiction writer, you will also be tempted by these fallacies. Appeal to authority, and popularity, personal attack, and emotionally fueled language are just four fallacies that are used often in journalism. Journalist will say things like "Janet was found dead in her lower east side apartment wearing a short leather mini skirt and a copious amount of face makeup". Journalist will give you completely irrelevant facts about a death, because they want you to come up with your own mislead, but exciting conclusion. Below is an article that was recently taken from Yahoo news.

SALT LAKE CITY - Houston's

FBI office has placed the fugitive daughter of a deceased Utah polygamist on the agency's "most wanted" list after getting a tip about the woman from a relative in prison. (** instructors notes: Notice how the author started this paragraph with the terms "fugitive daughter". This is the logical fallacy guilt by association. He also tells of her fathers sexual preference being "polygamist" (meaning having more than one sexual partner), to make you think that this persons morals are below the average American moral standard. This too is a logical fallacy because it has nothing to do with the daughter who is in question. It is simply emotionally fueled language that both confuses cause and effect, makes a "hasty generalization" that because a father had a certain moral standard, so will his daughter" and accuses the daughter of guilt by association by informing that her father was a fugitive. This first paragraph alone should make you see how logical fallacies make for exciting writing, but from a journalism standpoint, weaken you as a writer. Moving on to the article again. (*** end of instructor comments). Jacqueline Tarsa LeBaron is wanted in connection with four 1988 murders in Houston and Irving, Texas, according to a wanted poster on the agency's Web site. She's been a fugitive since 1992.

A telephone message left by The Associated Press with the Houston FBI office was not returned Saturday. (*** instructor's comments: Here is an example of an appeal to emotion. They again are trying to lead you to believe that non returned phone call is proof of guilt).

LeBaron is a daughter of Ervil LeBaron, the former leader of the Church of the Lamb of God, a polygamist sect with enclaves in Mexico.

The elder LeBaron ordered the executions of rival polygamists in the 1970s, investigators have said. In 1972 he was convicted in Utah of ordering family members to kill his brother, who was said to have disobeyed church laws.

Ervil LeBaron died in the Utah state prison in 1981. Before his death, he reportedly wrote a "bible" which included a commandment to kill disobedient church members.

It was also rumored that he left behind a "hit list" and that some of his 54 children were carrying out his commands.

Jacqueline LeBaron is one of six LeBaron family members charged with the June 1988 murders of three men who chose to leave the sect and the 8-year-old daughter of one victim. Each was shot in the head with a shotgun.

In 1995, three of the accused killers were convicted and sentenced to life in prison. Another was convicted of ordering the deaths and was sentenced to 45 years in prison. The youngest, who was 16 at the time of the murders, pleaded guilty to killing the child and served five years in prison.

Houston FBI special agent Todd Burns said there is renewed interest in Jacqueline LeBaron because a half brother who claims to have had a religious conversion in prison came forward with new information.

"He said they had an agreement to meet in Mexico. At one time they talked about meeting there before they got arrested and that never took place," Burns said. "He claims to not know anything about her whereabouts or whether she's living." Authorities believe Jacqueline LeBaron, who has worked as an English teacher, is in Mexico, where she was born and where the family had several polygamist colonies. (End of article)

As you can see, the above article is filled with logical fallacies. Does it make the article more interesting? Probably. Does it make the article right? Not necessarily.

ASSIGNMENT

So you can become better aware of what a logical fallacy is I will present a story here where your assignment is to find the logical fallacies in the article.

Logical fallacies happen all the time in different types of news, especially crime stories, as wells as health stories. This example was printed from The Washington Post on August 29, 2005 and is titled "Just Check the ID" by Sally Jenkins

Just Check the ID
By Sally Jenkins

Monday, August 29, 2005; Page E01

Athletes do things that seem transcendental -- and they can also do things that are transcendentally stupid. They choke, trip and dope. Nevertheless, they possess a deep physical knowledge the rest of us can learn from, bound as we are by our ordinary, trudging, cumbersome selves. Ever get the feeling that they are in touch with something that we aren't? What is that thing? Could it be their random, mutant talent, or could it be evidence of, gulp, intelligent design?

The sports section would not seem to be a place to discuss intelligent design, the notion that nature shows signs of an intrinsic intelligence too highly organized to be solely the product of evolution. It's an odd intersection, admittedly. You might ask, what's so intelligently designed about ballplayers (or sportswriters)? Jose Canseco once let a baseball hit him in the head and bounce over the fence for a home run. Former Washington Redskins quarterback Gus Frerotte gave himself a concussion by running helmet-first into a wall in a fit of exuberance. But athletes also are explorers of the boundaries of physiology and neuroscience, and some intelligent design proponents therefore suggest they can be walking human laboratories for their theories.

First, let's get rid of the idea that ID (intelligent design) is a form of sly creationism. It isn't. ID is unfairly confused with the movement to teach creationism in public schools. The most serious ID proponents are complexity theorists, legitimate scientists among them, who believe that strict Darwinism and especially neo-Darwinism (the notion that all of our qualities are the product of random mutation) is inadequate to explain the high level of organization at work in the world. Creationists are attracted to ID, and one its founding fathers, University of California law professor Phillip Johnson, is a devout Presbyterian. But you don't have to be a creationist to think there might be something to it, or to agree with Johnson when he says, "The human body is packed with marvels, eyes and lungs and cells, and evolutionary gradualism can't account for that."

The idea, so contentious in other contexts, actually rings a loud bell in sports. Athletes often talk of feeling an absolute fulfillment of purpose, of something powerful moving through them or in them that is not just the result of training. Jeffrey M. Schwartz, a neuroscientist and research professor of psychiatry at the UCLA School of Medicine, is a believer in ID, or as he prefers to call it, "intrinsic intelligence." Schwartz wants to launch a study of NASCAR drivers, to better understand their extraordinary focus. He finds Darwinism, as it applies to a high-performance athlete such as Tony Stewart, to be problematic. To claim that Stewart's mental state as he handles a high-speed car "is a result of nothing more than random processes coming together in a machine-like way is not a coherent explanation," Schwartz said.

Instead, Schwartz theorizes that when a great athlete focuses, he or she may be "making a connection with something deep within nature itself, which lends itself to deepening our intelligence." It's fascinating thought. And Schwartz would like to prove it's scientifically justifiable.

Steve Stenstrom, who played quarterback for the Bears and 49ers, works as a religious-life adviser to athletes at Stanford, where he organized a controversial forum on intelligent design last May. "I don't think it's a reach at all," he said. "Talk to any athlete, and if they really are honest, they realize that while they have worked and trained, and put a lot of effort into being great, they started with some raw material that was advantageous to them, and that it was meant to work a certain way. We all recognize that we have a certain design element."

A strict Darwinist would suggest this is an illusion and point out that there are obvious flaws in the body. Peter Weyand, a researcher in kinesiology and biomechanics at Rice University, observes, "Humans in the realm of the animal kingdom aren't terribly athletic."

Racehorses are much faster, and, for that matter, so are hummingbirds. We seem to have a basic quest to go higher, farther, faster -- one of our distinguishing features is that we push our limits for a reason other than survival, and construct artificial scales of achievement -- but we have some built-in debility. Human muscle can only get so strong; it will only produce as much force as it has area, about 3.5 kilograms of weight per square centimeter. "We're endowed with what we have by virtue of evolution, and it's not like engineering where we can pick materials and throw out what doesn't work," Weyand said.

Our bodies break down a lot. If we were designed more intelligently, presumably we wouldn't have osteoporosis or broken hips when we get old. Some evolutionists suppose that the process, through which people evolved from four-legged creatures to two, has had negative orthopedic consequences.

We are flawed cardiovascular. Horses carry much more oxygen in their blood, and have a storage system for red blood cells in their spleens, a natural system of blood doping. Humans don't. Also, while a lot of aerobics can make our hearts bigger, our lungs are unique. They don't adapt to training. They're fixed. We're stuck with them, and can only envy the antelopes.

None of which satisfies Schwartz, or Stenstrom. "I don't think we can attach athletic design to 'better' design," Stenstrom said. ". . . Some people are designed with an ear for music, others with a capacity to think deep thoughts about the world."

Schwarz finds little or nothing in natural selection to explain the ability of athletes to reinterpret physical events from moment to moment, the super-awareness that they seem to possess. He has a term for it, the ability to be an "impartial spectator" to your own actions. "The capacity to stand outside yourself and be aware of where you are," he said. "Deep within the complexities of molecular organization lays an intrinsic intelligence that accounts for that deep organization, and is something that we can connect with through the willful focus of our minds," he theorizes.

Crackpot speculation? Maybe -- maybe not. ID certainly lacks a body of scientific data, and opponents are right to argue that the idea isn't developed enough to be taught as equivalent to evolution. But Darwin himself admitted he didn't know everything about everything. "When I see a tail feather on a peacock, it makes me sick," he once said, before he understood it was for mating. And try telling a baseball fan that pure Darwinism explains Joe DiMaggio. As Tommy Lasorda once said, "If you said to God, 'Create someone who was what a baseball player should be,' God would have created Joe DiMaggio -- and he did."

None of this is to say that we shouldn't be wary of the uses for which ID might be hijacked. In the last year, numerous states have experienced some sort of anti-evolution movement. That makes it all the more important for the layman to distinguish the various gradations between evolutionists, serious scientists who are interested in ID, "neo-Creos," and Biblical literalists. One of the things we learn in a grade school science class is a concrete way of thinking, a sound, systematic way of exploring the natural world.

But science class also teaches us how crucial it is to maintain adventurousness, and surely it's worthwhile to suggest that an athlete in motion conveys an inkling of something marvelous in nature that perhaps isn't explained by mere molecules. Johann Kepler was the first to accurately plot the laws of planetary motion. But he only got there because he believed that their movements, if translated musically, would result in a celestial harmony. He also believed in astrology. And then there was Albert Einstein, who remarked that "Science without religion is lame; religion without science is blind." Historically, scientific theorists are sandlot athletes, drawing up plays in the dirt.

Good luck with the assignment!

CHAPTER 5

ELEMENTS OF THE ART AND CRAFT OF WRITING

Hello and welcome to chapter five on the elements of the art and craft of writing. Here's where the juicy stuff starts. This is the fun part.

The elements of the art and craft of writing we will be covering:

- Tips on keeping it simple
- Importance of dictionaries and thesauri
- Tips on writing with your "true" voice and narration
- Overview of possible angles and points of view

Tips on keeping it simple

- In general, avoid words with "ion" at the end
- Always look for the simple ways of saying things. When you feel like saying "at this moment," write "now."
- Use writing guides to help you keep your language clean – meaning uncluttered (like my office at the moment)
- Read children's books, newspapers, magazines and a lot of traditional, as well as alternative journalism. Surf the 'net and read the content for style. This is where you will find a sense of getting your meaning across quickly
- After you finish writing, edit yourself (we'll go into more detail about this later)
- Read your copy out loud. If you stumble on a word, it probably doesn't fit and needs editing
- Always choose the short word over the long word. In the world of writing non-fiction "short words have reason to live."

For more information on vocabulary use, check out: www.balancedreading.com/vocabulary.html. The website is presented by Dr. Sebastian Wren and here are some words from the site:

> If you are reading this, chances are you are a habitual reader, meaning you read on average an hour or two a day. As such, I can say with some authority, that most of the words you know, you learned through the act of reading. Research has shown that past the 4th grade, the number of words a person knows depends primarily on how much time they spend reading (Hayes & Ahrens, 1988; Nagy & Anderson, 1984; Nagy & Herman, 1987; Stanovich, 1986). In fact, by the time they reach adulthood, people who make a habit of reading have a vocabulary that is about four times the size of those who rarely or never read. This disparity starts early and grows throughout life....
>
> According to Beck and McKeown (1991), 5 to 6 year olds have a working vocabulary of 2,500 to 5,000 words. Whether a child is near the bottom or the top of that range depends upon their literacy skills coming into the first grade (Graves,1986; White, Graves & Slater, 1990). In other words, by the first grade, the vocabulary of the disadvantaged student is half that of the advantaged student, and over time, that gap widens.
>
> The average student learns about 3,000 words per year in the early school years -- that's 8 words per day (Baumann & Kameenui, 1991; Beck & McKeown, 1991; Graves, 1986), but vocabulary growth is considerably worse for disadvantaged students than it is for advantaged students (White, Graves & Slater, 1990). How important is vocabulary size? Imagine how much harder your life would be if you didn't understand 75% of the words you currently know. How hard would it be to read a passage of text if you didn't know many of the words in the passage? Imagine if reading the front page of the newspaper was like reading this passage of text:
>
> *"While shortening efrades the populace of the vaderbee class, most experts concur that a scrivant rarely endeavors to decry the ambitions and shifferings of the moulant class. Deciding whether to oxant the blatantly maligned Secting party, most moulants will tolerate the subjugation of staits, savats, or tempets*

only so long as the scrivant pays tribute to the derivan, either through preem or exaltation."

Would you read the newspaper if it was all like that? Would you read anything you didn't have to? Most non-readers have difficulty decoding the individual words, but in addition, even if they can decode them, most non-readers do not understand many of the words in formal text.

Wren goes onto to say expanding one's vocabulary is a lifelong effort in learning. However, although you may learn many "big" words, try to keep it simple in the art of communication so you can get your points across.

Wren also recommends Steven Stahl's book *Vocabulary Development*. As he puts it, "this is a very short but highly informative book that describes research findings and has suggestions for classroom instruction."

Importance of dictionaries and thesauri

For many of you, English may not be your first language. For others, it's your native tongue. Whatever the case, a dictionary and thesaurus always comes in handy.

An acquaintance of mine and I were talking about the fact most humans when it comes to language, especially the English language, only use a small portion of the vocabulary that is available.

When you are writing your creative non-fiction pieces, try to use simple words you often don't. A dictionary and thesaurus comes in extremely handy in this case.

I've heard of people who have read the entire dictionary. This is an awesome accomplishment, especially for people whom really want to become wordsmiths. As a writer, it helps to be a wordsmith; however, if you have the necessary tools, this will help in making your writing rich and colourful.

Think of the writing in this piece from David Remnick's *Life Stories* as an example of wonderful writing when it comes to vocabulary. This selection comes from

"The Soloist" and is a profile of famed Russian ballet dancer Mikhail Baryshnikov by Joan Acocella:

> What has made Baryshnikov a paragon of late-twentieth-century dance is partly the purity of his ballet technique. In him the hidden meaning of ballet, and of classicism – that experience has order, that life can be understood – is clearer than in any other dancer on the stage today. Another part of his preeminence derives, of course, from his virtuosity, the lengths to which he was able to take ballet – the split leaps, the cyclonic pirouettes – without sacrificing purity. But what has made him an artist, and a poplar artist, is the completeness of his performances: the level of concentration, the fullness of the jaw, even the splay of the fingers, all deployed in the service of a single, pressing act of imagination. In him there is simply more to see than in most other dancers. No matter what role his is playing (and he has played some thankless ones), he always honors it completely, working every minute to make it a serious human story. In an interview prior to the Riga concerts, the Latvian theatre critic Normunds Naumanis asked him why he danced. He answered that he was not a religious person (quickly adding that his mother had been, and he had him secretly baptized) but that he thought he found onstage what people seek in religion: "some approximation to exaltation, inner purification, self-discovery." He may hate interviews, but once he is in one he tends to pour his heart out. (This may be why he hates them).

Acocella has used a rich array of language. Everything from where she starts with the word "paragon," to the phrases like "cyclonic pirouettes," to the last two sentences, it is a well-crafted paragraph. Does it make you want to read the whole thing? I bet it does.

ASSIGNMENT 5.1

These are 25 unusual words and phrases which you need to place into 25 sentences which you will create. There are also 9 phrases that you need to recreate and make your own by making full sentences out of them. This is a really fun assignment. Best of luck.

1. Mocker – He was a mocker of the standards of his society
2. Emulate – He tried to emulate his brothers character

3. Piety – He had a distain for established pieties.
4. Conjecture – He gave raise to strange conjecture
5. Obscurity – he indulged in his cravings for opium and obscurity
6. Vileness – the very vileness of thief and outcast
7. Parity – suggesting a close parity between the realms.
8. Duplicity – he suggested that duplicity is an essential part of existence.
9. Debauchery – indulging in debauchery
10. Depiction – an accurate depiction of the male role within society.
11. Articulates – Shannon articulates a version of her story worth hearing.
12. Cynical – he was a very cynical man.
13. Conceit – it is a powerful and disturbing conceit.
14. unbridled – unbridled indulgence in pleasures
15. Promptly – the event was promptly cancelled.
16. Marvelous – it was a marvelous speech
17. Adore – I adore good music.
18. Tawdry – I looked out on the performance. It was a tawdry affair.
19. Prudence – she told me to exercising prudence when crossing the river.
20. Desolate – the scene was depressing and desolate
21. Inclined – I'm inclined think this was the best decision of my life.
22. Vivacious – she had a vivacious aura about her
23. Irrevocable – marriage is an irrevocable vow.
24. Transfigured – she was transfigured with joy
25. Sphere – he spoke about the ideas as if they belonged to two separate spheres of thought.

Phrases

1. Blurring the distinction between rich and poor.
2. Constraints of social conformity
3. The provoked and outraged response
4. Some of these views help to illuminate my point
5. To even enter into the realm of debate on these issues shows your lack of humility.
6. Lay there in a frightened pleasure.
7. Working long hours robs the color of the human heart.
8. The business venture seemed to promise rich and fruitful results.

9. I'm interested in the intersection between freedom and companionship.

Have fun! I know did coming up with the words and phrases. Upload your completed sentences to your personal website.

Tips on writing with your "true" voice and narration

One of the things I find extremely helpful when I'm writing is my MD recorder. My MD recorder is a mini-disk (MD) device that allows me to record sound in digital format.

I've used this device for years, ever since I was doing freelance reporting for CBC Radio. Even with the added writing and teaching experience I've gained, I still find it useful. It can be a huge bother to be in an interview with someone and accurately take notes with your hands and a pad of paper. Most people don't write as fast as people talk in this age of the computer. Of course, it also helps to be able to type fast so if you're having a phone interview, you can keep track of what your source is saying. We'll get into interviewing later, but now I'll just capture the principles behind this writing tool which can help everyone from a beginner to a pro.

Another tip to writing in a plain style is to write the way you speak. This is best captured by talking to the microphone, recording your voice and telling the story you're working on. After you've done that, you can transcribe the tape – there's lots of work for writers in transcription – and shape the story with quotes from sources. This will best help to distinguish your "true" voice from the voice of your sources.

Theordore A. Rees Cheney whom is the author of *Writing Creative Nonfiction*, discusses the importance of voice starting on page 130. She uses an example from Lewis H. Lapham, editor of Harper's magazine. The example comes from a 1983 piece called "On Reading" in his column "Notebook":

> On first opening a book I listen for the sound of the human voice. By this device I am absolved from reading much of what is published in a given year. Most writers make use of institutional codes (academic, literary, political, bureaucratic, and technical), in which they send messages already deteriorating into the half-life of yesterday's news. Their transmissions remain largely unintelligible, and un-

less I must decipher them for professional reasons, I am content to let them pass by. I listen, instead, for a voice in which I can hear the music of the human improvisation as performed through 5,000 years on the stage of recorded time.

....As a student, and later as an editor and occasional writer of reviews, I used to feel obliged to finish every book I began to read. This I no longer do. If within the first few pages I cannot hear the author's voice....I abandon him at the first convenient opportunity.

This shows how important it is to inject your own voice into your writing. Don't be afraid to express who you really are and this will come through in your writing.

You may need to structure the transcription with the combination of your voice written and the quotes you've received from your sources. Refer back to chapter two to recall basic story-telling techniques.

Darlene Maciuba-Koppel in *The Web Writer's Guide: Tips & Tools* quotes from William Zinsser who wrote the classic book called *On Writing Well*. Zinsser says "You learn to write by writing." Maciuba-Koppel also believes this statement is true for the web as well. I actually have the statement "Just write it" under my name on my own website at: www.donnakakonge.com.

Finding one's writing voice can be tricky at first, but the cure is to keep practicing. I once spoke to a lawyer that has 40 years of experience in law. He said the interesting thing about his job is he was still *practicing* law. The same is true of writing. Even great ones like Margaret Atwood, Dionne Brand, Robertson Davies, Wole Soyinka, Ralph Ellison – and these are examples of fiction writers – however, the craft of storytelling is still the same principle.

Along that vein of learning by doing, here's an assignment just for you students.

ASSIGNMENT 5.2

One of the easiest ways to find your voice through writing is by starting with your own oral voice. Many of us write the way we talk.

Get a tape recorder, or some type of recording device and tell a story – talk about the events of your day. This type of story-telling is also known as "a day in the life" type of stories.

Then, transcribe the story into a word processing document and post to your personal website on I.

Do not edit the piece before you hand it in. The purpose of this exercise is to discover your true voice.

Overview of possible angles and points of view

With traditional journalism, there are so many stories which come out where the same one is covered by various media publications. In order to be different from the competition, often it's the angle, or point of view, which can sell or sink a newspaper or magazine. This is especially true of the cover stories. Angles or points of view are also known as the "slant" of a story.

Angle and/or point of view, is the approach the writer takes to a story. For example, if I were writing a story about milk. One approach or possible angle may be to write about how it can help fight bone cancer, turning it into a health story. Another approach may be to discuss how the price of milk has skyrocketed over the past 15 years – this would make it a business story.

The same is true in creative non-fiction. We'll discuss two types: objective and subjective. There are a variety of angles and points of view the writer – you – can take. Here's an overview, which will be followed by explanations and descriptions:

- Objective: opinions and judgments are not included in this style of writing. Many examples can be found in any most newspapers you read in democratic newspapers. Here's one of the objective approach taken from *The Toronto Star* titled "Swim coach scandal spurs calls for review" by Heba Aly and Richard Brennan:

> An ex-convict with a history of drug trafficking has no business coaching children in competitive swimming and should be stripped of his duties, Ontario Progressive Conservative Leader John Tory said yesterday.

And respected former Canadian Olympic athlete Bruce Kidd said if Cecil Russell, 53, was instructing his children he would pull them out of the swim club.

Reaction to Russell having his lifetime coaching ban lifted by the Canadian Centre for Ethics in Sports, as reveal in a front page Toronto Star story yesterday, had been met with shock to muted indifference, especially by the federal government. The controversy has sparked calls for more regulation of coaches.

Russell, twice arrested for trafficking of steroids and ecstasy, who also testified he helped burn and dispose of a dismembered body, is now running Oakville's Dolphins Swim Club.

The reporters decided the focus of their story was to cover the reaction to the reinstating of the ex-convict swim coach. They don't include any of their personal opinions, only the opinions of others to gather their information.

- Subjective: This approach is when the writer decides to infuse their personal opinion into the written piece. Here's an example *The Globe of Mail* of July 24, 2006. The writer is John Coo and the piece appeared on the Facts & Arguments page titled, "Summertime and the clothing is breezy":

There were advantages to this dressed-down uniform. But saying so is mere rationalization for my licentious behaviour. The onset of hot weather sets young men to thinking about.....summer dress-down days. As a callow youth, I always had clear views on "casual Fridays" – they were a bad thing; an indicator of the moral and sartorial laxness of modern society. I had always been of the school of thought that says "If you have a job, you wear a suit and tie." End of story. I suppose I was prepared to bend so far as to modify this philosophy to read "sports coat and tie" for advertising copy writers, plainclothes policemen and university professors. And if you are dressed in a suit, then you wear the jacket, always.

In this piece by Coo, he injects his personal opinion. He takes a subjective view point. His slant is subjective.

Conclusion

The elements of the art and craft of writing are many, but the ones covered in this chapter include a plain writing style, language usage and vocabulary expansion and the two main approaches you can take to your writing.

Keep in mind this chapter involves those things you do while writing, however, having a clear plan before writing is important, especially when it comes to the angle you will take, so you don't write in a confusing manner by switching back and forth between points of view. Organizing your time and yourself as a writer will be discussed in chapter nine.

ASSIGNMENT

Write two, one page stories, using an objective slant with one and a subjective slant with the other. You can look through your local newspaper and take a story that is controversial and in one page, practice objectivity – finding sources and doing research that will present a balanced point of view from your perspective. With the second part of the assignment, write an opinion piece (your opinion). The only research will come from your knowledge of the story and clearly outlining your opinions on the story and supporting your arguments with facts. Keep in mind the points raised in this chapter and include the elements in your writing.

Post your assignment to your personal website for my review.

CHAPTER 6

IMPORTANCE OF NARRATION AND DIALOGUE

Hello and welcome to chapter six on the importance of narration and dialogue. Let's make sure you understand this well and if you have any questions, let's keep the spirit of dialogue alive and post your questions to your personal website and don't forget to e-mail me so I know you've posted to your website.

Discussing narration brings us back to discussions about voice, although I will concentrate on different elements in this chapter. Good dialogue is like the spice to your stew – it can make your story extremely palatable.

We'll begin with a discussion on narration with reference taken from *Guide to Writing Magazine Nonfiction* by Michael J. Bugeja. This excerpt is on page 103 of the book:

Magazine writers need all the time they can get – not only to meet deadlines but also to convey to readers the *reality* of an experience. If a subjective truth is significant, narrating it via the elements of grammatical, chronological, and literary time enchants or engages the audience, allowing readers to immerse themselves in a work. That's why magazines are visually powerful. The medium was interactive long before webzines on the Internet.

Bugeja goes on to say writers use narration so the reader can relate to what you know. These moments of narration are determined by the following criteria:

• **Content**. Will you share your own or a source's personal experience? Or will you or your source speak as expert without mentioning the personal experience at all? Or will you do both, sharing the impact of experience and the insight of expertise?

• **Expression of content.** Will you put the readers on the scene, recounting events chronologically as if they were happening before the readers' eyes? Or will you articulate your truths without any sense of plot (time line) or chronology, as if you were conversing with readers or sharing your opinions? Or will you do both, recounting events so readers can envision them first and analyze them later?

- **Structure**. By answering the preceding questions, you can outline a story according to events associated with it or insights emanating out t – step by step, point by point.

The above outline helps you to think about some things in making decisions about when narration is appropriate in a story, or when you may choose to let your sources tell the story. We'll have an assignment later on where you will have a chance to practice these elements. For now, we'll continue by discussing important elements such as the use of tenses while writing your narration.

The following is not a grammar chapter; however, the tense you choose to use in your narration is important to how it will be perceived by the reader. Here's an example from George Plimpton's "How to Face a Firing Squad," which first appeared in *Esquire*. He originally wrote it in the past tense, but Bugeja has also written it in the present and future tenses so you can compare how it affects narration:

Past Tense

In the early hours of December 22, 1849, Fyodor Dostoyevsky was led out to the Semyonvsky parade ground in St. Petersburg to be executed by a firing squad. He was twenty-seven at the time. The crime had committed was the "attempt to disseminate writings against the government by means of a hand printing press." Twenty others – poets, teachers, officers, journalists had been sentenced with him. The procedure was that they would die in groups of three. Dostoyevsky was in the second group.

It was a monstrous hoax, of course, initiated by Nicholas I, known with good reason as the Iron Czar. Just as the adjutant in charge of the firing squad was to lower his saber and shout "Fire!" one of the czar's aides-de-camp galloped across the parade ground and handed the officer a sealed packet that contained commutations of sentence. According to a historian friend of mine, these were read out at agonizing length by an officer known as the worst stutterer in the Russian army. Dostoyevsky was sentenced to four years of penal servitude.

I looked all this up the other day because I had a luncheon date with Larry Rivers, the well-known painter, who during the civil unrest in Nigeria some time ago went through a similar, if not quite as dramatic, experience. How often does one have lunch with a man who has survived a firing squad?

Present Tense

In the early hours of December 22, 1849, Fyodor Dostoyevsky is led out to the Semyonovsky parade ground in St. Petersburg to be executed by a firing squad. He is twenty-seven at the time. The crime he has committed is the "attempt to disseminate writings against the government by means of a hand printing press." Twenty others – poets, teachers, officers, journalists have been sentenced with him. The procedure is that they will die in groups of three. Dostoyevsky is in the second group.

It is a monstrous hoax, of course, initiated by Nicholas I, known with good reason as the Iron Czar. Just as the adjutant in charge of the firing squad is to lower his saber and shout "Fire!" one of the czar's aides-de-camp galloped across the parade ground and hands the officer a sealed packet that contained commutations of sentence. According to a historian friend of mine, these are read out at agonizing length by an officer known as the worst stutterer in the Russian army. Dostoyevsky is sentenced to four years of penal servitude.

I looked all this up the other day because I have a luncheon date with Larry Rivers, the well-known painter, who during the civil unrest in Nigeria some time ago went through a similar, if not quite as dramatic, experience. How often does one have lunch with a man who has survived a firing squad?

Future Tense

In the early hours of December 22, 1849, Fyodor Dostoyevsky will be led out to the Semyonovsky parade ground in St. Petersburg to be executed by a firing squad. He will be twenty-seven at the time. The crime he will have committed is the "attempt to disseminate writings against the government by means of a hand printing press." Twenty others – poets, teachers, officers, journalists will have been sentenced with him. The procedure is that they will die in groups of three. Dostoyevsky will be in the second group.

It will be a monstrous hoax, of course, initiated by Nicholas I, known with good reason as the Iron Czar. Just as the adjutant in charge of the firing squad is to lower his saber and shout "Fire!" one of the czar's aides-de-camp will have galloped across the parade ground and hands the officer a sealed packet that contained commutations of sentence. According to a historian friend of mine, these will be read out at agonizing length by an officer known as the worst stutterer in the Russian army. Dostoyevsky will be sentenced to four years of penal servitude.

Students note: I'm not going to include the last sentence of this story because it sounds confusing in the future tense.

The basic information does not change, however, the tone of the articles change written through different tenses of narration.

The tenses of a story affect the general understanding to the reader. The past tense tends to give a more "historical" light to the piece. The present tense is often favoured in creative non-fiction writing because it's seen as more "lively" and "current." The future tense is basically a writing style based on promises that may or may not be kept.

Think about your life. The things which have happened are past tense, or history. Think about the things currently happening. This is present tense. Hopefully, it's lively, or at least enjoyable. Perhaps it would make for a good memoir or personal essay. Think about your future – which may or may not be certain regardless of your intentions. However, the future tense is one of those powerful resources writer's have because they can shed some light as to how a situation may play out. This is particularly good in the case of analysis and reviews.

To the reader, the tense you use will affect their state of mind and either put them in the past, present or the future. If you use these devices interchangeably, use them carefully. A movie like Momento (2002) is an excellent example of this device being used brilliantly in story-telling.

In a creative non-fiction piece, the best ones contain the same fundamentals you would also find in fiction stories – the differences are the non-fiction piece is based on facts. Some of the elements will be explained here.

More elements of story writing

Plot - Every good story needs a plot. A plot is the foundation of the story-telling thread. Movies like The Sound of Music have a plot of a young nun falling in love with a baron and his children while she works for him. Your stories will have a plot as well.

Character – After the plot comes the protagonist. In the case of The Sound of Music, the protagonist is the Julie Andrews character Maria. She is the main character in the plot. For your non-fiction pieces, it will be your extraordinary writing skills that will introduce your protagonist, as well as other interesting characters to the plot.

The goal with character development is every writer, including you, wants to make the reader feel like they know this person. You must add as much detail as you think of – appeal to all the senses. What kind of clothes does this person wear? What's their favourite drink? What's the first thing they do in the morning? etc. You want the reader to really understand and know your characters – especially the main characters and sources of your creative non-fiction pieces.

Here is some more information from a book that discusses story-telling from a digital media perspective, but is still relevant to creative non-fiction writing. It's called *Digital Storytelling: a creator's guide to interactive entertainment* by Carolyn Handler Miller:

> The two classic characters, the must-haves of every work of linear storytelling, originated in the classic Greek theatre. The first is the protagonist, our hero. This character is the central figure of the drama, whose mission, goal, or objective provides the story with its forward momentum. The second is the antagonist, the adversary who stands in the way of the protagonist, and whose opposition gives heat to the drama and provides the story with exciting conflict.
>
> Characteristics of Protagonists

Many authorities in drama, beginning with Aristotle, have contended that the most interesting characters are not perfect. In classic Greek theatre, as with Shakespeare's plays, the main characters are afflicted by what is often termed "a tragic flaw." Though noble in many ways, they also possess some weakness – jealousy, self-doubt, and ambition – a trait that leads to their undoing. In lighter stories protagonists usually have flaws, too, though of a less serious nature. These dings in their personality will not lead to tragic consequences, but will often cause them trouble, and can also be the source of comic moments. Not every protagonist in interactive media has a flaw or a quirk, but such weaknesses are not uncommon....

What all protagonists do need are qualities that make them likable, believable, and attractive enough for you to want to spend time in their company. We need to understand why they have chosen to go after the particular goal the y are seeking – their passion to do this must make sense to us. After all, we must be able to identify with them. In other words, we need to be able to imagine ourselves in their position and feel what they are feeling.

Miller continues by discussing the antagonist. She mentions the antagonist is that person or thing that opposes the protagonist from reaching their goal. It is this type of conflict and finding the right sources to express these concepts in creative non-fiction that will turn your stories from good to great. Do keep these things in mind which Miller notes:

....opposition can also come from natural forces, such as violent storms, or from physical challenges, such as negotiating a boot camp obstacle. Opposition may also come from nonhuman threats, such as the spiders, snakes, and alligators....

Even humourous opponents fill an important function:

- They help sharpen the conflict.
- They supply obstacles.
- They pit the protagonist against a force that is easy to comprehend.

Keep in mind Miller is writing about interactive media, so many of your creative non-fiction stories may not have many spiders, snakes or alligators in them. However, if your protagonist has a fear of these things, that may make for an interesting creative non-fiction in itself. You may also have a number of antagonists in your story that your protagonist has to deal with.

Miller goes on to discuss techniques for developing digital characters that can also be employed when fully developing and writing your characters for your creative non-fiction pieces:

1. Probe deeply: Invest time in working out the character's backstory and psychological profile. What kind of family he or she is from and what kind of upbringing and schooling did he or she receive? Is the character from a small town or a big city? What are the special skills and talents of this person, and what are the kinds of things he or she simply can't or won't do? What is the romantic and marital history of the character? What is your character most afraid of? What does the character most hope for? Though you may never use most of this information, it will help you develop a rich and interesting character, and sometimes a small detail will give you just the inspiration you need to give the character a unique and unforgettable touch.

2. Motivate the character: What is it the character is striving for in this narrative? Why is it so important? Each character should have a goal, not just the protagonist and the antagonist. The motivation should be something this is easy to understand and doesn't require much explaining.

3. Make the character vivid: interactive media does not leave any room for subtlety [neither does creative non-fiction writing]. The user needs to be able to "read" the character quickly – to understand the essence of that character. The character's most important traits should shine through clearly and should not be blurred by too much detail or by contradictory personality clues. Thus, you need to decide what essential things you want to project about each character and focus on those. For a model, look at comic strips, comic books, and animated movies, all of which do a good job of using shorthand techniques to convey characters.

4. Avoid stereotypes, or alternatively, play against them: When you have limited time or methods to reveal who your character is, it is extremely tempting to fall in to the use of stereotypes. Yes, the participants will be able to quickly recognize the thick-necked bully, the eccentric scientist, and the gossipy next door neighbour. But they will just as quickly yawn, because stereotypes make your work seem

predictable and bland. It is much more interesting to take a stereotype and twist it. How about a thick-necked bully who has a tender spot for little old ladies? Or making the eccentric scientist a little girl? Or having the friendly next door neigbour is mute?

8. Use dialogue to help convey personality: Dialogue can do more than impart information; it can reveal information about the character's personality, background, and occupation.

Miller also makes some powerful suggestions on ways of revealing character in your writing that can apply to creative non-fiction:

1. Their physical appearance: this includes not only their face and body, but also how they dress and how they move.
2. What the say...
3. Their interactions with other characters: The way characters act with each other can reveal a great deal about their emotions and feelings for each other.
4. What they do: Behaviour can indicate emotional states like anxiety, anger, and sorrow. It can also indicate slyness and the readiness to be aggressive.
5. What other characters tell us: We can learn about a character's history from what other characters say about them.

Theme – The theme of a story like *The Sound of Music* is basically "love conquers all." In Truman Capote's *In Cold Blood*, the theme is murder and justice. Your stories will equally have a theme to them which will most likely develop naturally; however, it's good to think about what you want as the theme of your story. Your focus statement will be helpful in developing the theme.

All these aspects of story development give the narrator – you – omniscient powers. You make the decisions as to how the story will be told. You may choose to structure the dialogue and narration (which strongly indicates character development) in the third person if you insert yourself into the story. You may choose to do it in the first person. However, you choose to do it, or experiment with different methods until you're satisfied with a particular story-telling structure – it's up to you.

The best to discover powerful narrative styles is to read as much as you can. You should be reading as many newspapers, magazines, books, seeing movies and reading online as much as possible.

The best way to understand theme is thinking about the media you like – what has been the general theme? When it comes to reality shows – in general the theme is people will do anything for money and fame. In Shakespeare's novels, he often exposed the underbelly of human nature. It's the overall impression you want to leave with the reader, which is quite different from the story-telling and strategic nature of plot development.

MID-CHAPTER ASSIGNMENT 6.1

Create a plot, character and a theme:

In this assignment you will be creating a plot, character and theme and using a real-life source to create a two-page story. First, start by interviewing your source – which is the basis for how many stories develop in creative non-fiction. From there you will naturally find the plot and theme.

Remember, if you find the character interesting, so will your reader and all the other elements of this assignment will fall into place.

Dialogue

Strong dialogue can help a reader love you and your writing. When collecting your research and doing the interviewing, which will be discussed in chapter seven, you don't need to use all of the information you gather. You need to be selective. You want to use the best parts. Here's an example from Cheney's *Writing Creative Nonfiction*. It's from the bestselling book *The Selling of the President* by Joe McGinnis about Richard M. Nixon:

> He took his position on the front of the heavy brown desk. He liked to lean against a desk, or sit on the edge of one, while he taped commercials, because he felt this made him seem informal. There were about twenty people, technicians and advisors, gathered in a semi-circle around the cameras. Richard Nixon looked at them and frown.
>
> "Now when we start," he said, "don't have anybody who is not directly involved in this in my range of vision. So I don't go shifting my eyes."

"Yes, sir." All right, clear the stage. Everybody who's not actually doing something get off the stage, please. Get off the stage."

There was one man in the corner, taking pictures. His flash blinked several times in succession. Richard Nixon looked his direction. The man had been hired by the Nixon staff to take informal pictures throughout the campaign for historical purposes.

Are they stills?" Richard Nixon said. "Are they our own stills? Well then, knock them off." He motioned with his arm.

"Can them. We've already got so goddamned many stills already." Richard Nixon turned back toward the cameras.

"Now, when you give me the fifteen-second cue, give it to me right under the camera so I don't shift my eyes."

"Right, sir."

Here's an example of letting pure conversation tell the story. It's from Gay Talese in a chapter called "The Soft Psyche of Joshua Logan" in his book *The Overreachers*:

Now he was back in the dark theatre, the lights of the stage beaming on the actors going through a scene in the garden of their Louisiana shack; Claudia McNeil's voice was now softer because she had had a touch of laryngitis a few days before. But at the end of the scene, she raised her voice to its full power, and Logan, in a pleasant tone, said, "Don't strain your voice, Claudia."

She did not respond, only whispered to another actor on stage.

"Don't raise your voice, Claudia," Logan repeated.

She again ignored him.

"Claudia!" Logan yelled, "don't you give me that actor's revenge, Claudia."

"Yes, Mr. Logan," she said with a soft sarcastic edge.

"I've had enough of this today, Claudia."

"Yes, Mr. Logan."

"And stop Yes – Mr. Logan-ing me."

"Yes, Mr. Logan."

"You're a shocking, rude woman!"

"Yes, Mr. Logan."

"You're being a beast."

"Yes, Mr. Logan."

"Yes, Miss Beast."

"Yes, Mr. Logan."

"Yes, Miss beast!"

Suddenly, Claudia McNeil stopped. It dawned on her that he was calling her a beast; now her face was grey and her eyes were cold, and her voice almost solemn as she said, "You....called....me....out....of...my....name!"

"Oh, God!" Logan smacked his forehead with his hand.

This conversation is one-of-a-kind. The character development and interest in the story is propelled by the dialogue.

Tips to using dialogue:

- Record conversations while you're reporting and transcribe your notes
- Avoid using "said" and "say" repeatedly after people make their statements. Use your dictionary to find other ways of expressing your subjects' statements. You also don't want to overuse the word "states." Some alternatives may be "explained," "expressed," "mumbled," etc. You want to try to capture how the person actually made their statement rather than always just writing they said this and that.
- Narration should also be used as the point where you enter the story to explain something further, always use when necessary and try not to overdue – unless this is a stylistic device you are striving for where there is little dialogue in a piece
- Remember dialogue is important because it gives more life to a piece
- Alternatively, if you a writer of great talent, lack of dialogue will display your extraordinary story-telling skills

Carolyn Miller in *Digital Storytelling* has some great things to add about dialogue:

Despite all these new ways of communicating, dialogue is still a supremely important tool in most forms of interactive entertainment [as well as creative non-fiction]. It is a tool that has been refined and shaped through centuries of use. Even Aristotle, in his typically pithy way, offered some good pointers on writing effective dialogue. In the *Poetics* (Chapter XI, Section 16), he explained that dialogue is "....the faculty of saying what is possible and pertinent in a given circumstance." In other words, the character's lines should be believable and reveal only what is possible for him or her to know. And the speech should not ramble; it should be focused on the matter at hand.

A little later (Chapter XI, Section 17), Aristotle goes on to say that the words an actor speaks should be expressive of his character, showing "....what kind of thing a man chooses or avoids." Thus, the words the character speaks should reflect his goals, and probably his fears as well. Aristotle's remarks on dialogue have stood the test of time, and are as applicable to interactive media as they were to Greek drama.

In addition to Aristotle, we can learn about dialogue from modern day screenwriters. One of the most valuable things they can teach us is to use dialogue sparingly, only when there is no other means of conveying the information. "Show," they advise, "don't tell." But when screenwriters do resort to dialogue, they make sure the exchanges are brisk and easy to understand. They use simple, clear words, knowing this is not the place to show off one's vocabulary. And they break the exchanges between characters into short, bite-sized pieces, because long speeches make an audience restless.

Here are some pointers on dialogue from Miller:

1. As Aristotle indicated, keep speeches focused. They should be short and to the point.
2. Do as screenwriters do, and use clear, simple words and informal language and grammar. Short sentences are preferable to long ones, and avoid complex sentence constructions. Don't let your characters deliver long blocks of speech.
3. The lines a character speaks should be "in character." In other words, what the character says should reflect his personality, his age, his mood, his educational level, his profession, his goals, and his point of view.
6. Read what you have written out loud, listening for inadvertent tongue twisters, awkward phrases, unnatural speech, and overly long lines. Then cut and polish.

Miller also gives some tips on adding written communications in your stories. I'm only including the points which apply to creative non-fiction writing:

1. If producing a document that one of the ...characters...wrote, the writing should be "in character"....
2. Keep the document short. People don't want to spend much time reading.
3. If writing an email, model the telegraphic style of real emails, and even include an emoticon or two.
4. In the same way, model any other specialized type of written communication – including Web pages, blogs, and newspaper articles – on real life examples. If you know anyone who works in that field, have that person read what you've written and give you feedback. Strive to make the piece of writing as authentic looking as possible. From a participant's point of view, part of the fun of stumbling across a...document is the sense that it [is]..."real."

Conclusion

Narration and dialogue are key elements in making your story great. Especially when it comes to dialogue, it's the actual process of interviewing and capturing conversations that can add life to your stories. This will be discussed more in chapter seven.

ASSIGNMENT

Write a two page story using the points discussed in this chapter on narration and dialogue. If you feel like you're having difficulty on how to introduce dialogue, try tape recording a conversation with you and a friend to get a sense of the flow of how dialogue works. Then, transcribe the dialogue. Add narration to help explain the dialogue. Post the assignment to your personal website for my review.

CHAPTER 7

INTERVIEWING

Wait for those unguarded moments. Relax the mood and, like the child dropping off to sleep, the subject often reveals his truest self.
Barbara Walters (1931-   )

Hello and welcome to chapter seven on interviewing. There is an art to interviewing and interviewing styles can take on many different styles. A quick overview will be outlined here:

- Face-to-face interview with tape recorder and note-taking
- Face-to-face interview with tape recorder
- Face-to-face interview with note-taking
- Telephone interview with typing notes
- Telephone interview with hand-written notes
- E-mail interviews
- Interviews on message boards and chat lines

As you can see, there is a variety of ways to do interviews. Some of these you will need tools like a tape recorder, mini-disc (MD), MP3 recorder or online Skype and VoIP software to download onto your computer with a headset.

What are Skype and VoIP? It's a recent invention where long distance calls can be made free by using a headset, a microphone and the speakers from your phone. This is especially handy for long-distance interviewing. Find out more about it by typing in those words at www.google.com.

It's relatively inexpensive; however, the person you're interviewing also needs to have the software and the tools to do the interview as well.

The main ways I do my interviews are with my MD, using headphones to make sure the interview is being recorded properly. Sometimes I take notes at the same time and this is advisable to prevent from equipment failures or problems. When doing these types interviews with electronic recording devices, you always want to make sure you have enough batteries and discs or tapes. This part is called thinking of the logistics and avoiding any technical problems that may arise.

Once I've done my interviews with the MD, I then transcribe my notes. This is helpful if you are a fast typist like I am. Practicing this can also increase your typing speed, which comes in handy if you're writing to deadline.

I also do telephone interviews and type my notes into a Microsoft Word document. For Mac users and Linux users, there is software you can use on those computers. There are also a number of recording devices which can help you to record a conversation over the telephone.

You need to check that your source agrees to the recording of the interview before you start.

Some of the drawbacks of transcribing your notes are that it can be time-consuming depending on how fast you type. However, since most creative non-fiction pieces don't have the same timeline as hard-news stories, this shouldn't be a concern. If you are under a tight timeline, recording the interview and taking notes at the same time is advisable. Then, you can use the notes to find the places in your recording that the most important so you can fast forward and rewind quickly.

I'm going to include some legal information about recording interviews. The information comes from Michael Meanwell's *The Wealthy Writer:*

Recording and the Law

There are legal obligations regarding electronic recording of conversations, including face-to-face and phone interviews.

In some countries, the law requires only one person (which can be the interviewer who is recording) to consent to the taping of a conversation with another.

This means that you do not need to advise the subject that you are taping the phone call.

U.S. federal law also requires only one-party consent; however, twelve states require consent from every person participating in the conversation. It's important to note that if you're telephoning, for example, from New York (which only requires one-party consent) but you are recording a conversation with a subject in California (which requires all-party consent), then you are legally obligated to advise and gain permission to tape the interview before commencing. If you do not, you could be in violation of your subject's state law, even though the recording is lawful in your own state. The same principle in applies when conducting international telephone interviews, where the laws in the subject's country require all-party notification.

Unlawful recordings can – and have – resulted in civil suits and even criminal prosecution. Whether conducting interstate or international interviews, it's best to operate on the safe side and presume that the more stringent law applies. Always be upfront with your subject and advise her that you wish to tape the interview before it begins, and get an "okay" on tape. (Meanwell, 263)

Before you Start

Before you start your interview and you have all the necessary gear in place and know the laws, the first thing you need to do is to prepare your questions. This is after you've done your research.

Many writers have different interviewing techniques. I've been doing journalism for so long that most of the time I have some questions in my head and basically go by my gut when I ask questions. This can only be done when you've already done a lot of research. However, it is highly advisable that you prepare questions when you're first starting out.

Remember that the keys to journalism questions include the five W's and the H:

- Who?
- What?

- Where?
- When?
- Why?
- And How?

When I was in journalism school, I was told there are no stupid questions and this is true. Don't be afraid to ask a question or write one down because you think it might make you look stupid. You may discover it's the best question you have.

Types of Questioning

There are two different types of questions: close-ended and open-ended questions.

Close-ended questions are usually the ones where it prompts the source to answer with a simple "yes" or "no." In general, these types of questions should be avoided when doing in-depth stories for creative non-fiction pieces. You want your subject to speak at length on something. If you find they are going on a bit too much about something you don't need to know about for your story, you can always find a polite way to interject, just as you would in a regular conversation.

Open-ended questions are the ones you want to strive for. These are the types where you are leaving it open for all kinds of responses and allow your source to speak freely. An example of an open-ended question:

- How would you make the world a better place?

An example of this kind of question as a close-ended question would be:

- Do you think this world is a better place?

As you can see, the different types of questioning styles lend themselves to prompting longer answers in the open-ended question and shorter answers in the close-ended question.

Close-ended questions can come in handy during interviewing for simply confirming facts. They can be useful in traditional journalism methods.

Warming Up Your Source

At the beginning of an interview, you may be speaking with someone you have met for the first time, spoken with the first time, or emailed for the first time – you still want to leave a good impression.

I suggest doing a preliminary interview with your subject to find out if they are a media-friendly or media-savvy person. By this I mean, you want someone who is a bit of a talker, has the "gift of gab" so to speak. If you end up with a source who doesn't really like talking, this will make your interview extremely difficult. Try to speak to the person first before arranging an interview.

Once you have the interview, some opening questions or a simple conversation will help to establish some sort of bond between you and the source. You want the person to feel comfortable with you, as Barbara Walters says. The more comfortable the person is, the more likely they will be to tell you things they may not have ever told anyone else.

When you're doing phone interviews, smile on the phone. This technique is useful because most people can hear a smile. As well, when it's a face-to-face interview, you also want to make use of your teeth and smile at your source to help put them at ease.

The Interview

Here are some things to keep in mind during the interviewing:

• You may need to rephrase and/or repeat your questions. Your source has every right to ask for this
• Avoid leading questions. An example of a leading question: You went down to the bar that night didn't you? Avoid these type of questions because you're leading your subject into something that may not be accurate

- Keep in mind the power of silence once interviewing. Once you've asked your question and your source doesn't reply right away – keep quiet – you'll amazed how many people will just start talking to fill the gap

Qualities of a Successful Interviewer

Here are some qualities outlined in the successful interviewer as stated in Meanwell's *The Wealthy Writer*:

- Attentiveness
- Trustworthiness
- Objectivity
- Flexibility
- Spontaneity
- Positive Personality

Here's also a checklist for success from Meanwell:

- Know your interviewee
- Know your questions
- Think like a reader
- Be courteous
- Stay outside
- Stay on course
- Go off with the tangent
- Take note
- Ask if there is anything else
- Finish the interview

I just want to add something about the second last point above. It's extremely important that near the end of the interview you ask your source if there is anything else they would like to say. You may get the opportunity to include whole bunch information you hadn't thought of.

Here are some final words on interview from the esteemed journalism school The Poynter Institute in the United States:

1. Shut up
2. Shut up some more
3. Work from a list of questions, but veer off
4. Shut up again
5. Get there early, stay late
6. Interview a person on his turf
7. Ask for tours (of a photo album, book or music collection, memorabilia, set of golf clubs, wine cellar, favorite crack house, old neighborhood)
8. Write down things you see, not just answers to questions
9. Use your notebook to show that you are conducting a formal interview
10. Put your notebook away near the end, but keep talking
11. If you've got time, hand around a person to watch and record his interactions with others
12. Ask the most important questions more than once and in different forms
13. Ask the "slam door" questions last –the types of questions people don't want to answer
14. Shut up
15. Fill out or copy your notes as quickly as possible.

MID-CHAPTER ASSIGNMENT 7.1

Transcribe the following audio and don't pause the audio – just keep writing whatever you can get down.

Now, we'll continue with interviewing....

Here is a sample of interviewing from The New New Journalism by Robert S. Boynton about creative non-fiction writers and how they organize their time. Keep in mind these are writers that spend years, at least months on their stories. The following is a selection from his interview with Richard Ben Cramer:

How do you conduct interviews?

When I go in to interview someone, I don't prepare any questions. And not only do I have no questions, I don't have a notebook – and if I *have* a notebook, I don't take it out of my pocket.

I just look at him and say, "Look, here's my situation...." And I explain my *problem*. When I was interviewing the presidential candidates I'd say, "You know what my problem is? I can't imagine the time when you say to yourself, 'It *ought* to be me.' Because *nobody* I've ever known would say something like that. So I want to know what you think *happened* that made you think 'It's got to be me'? What was the last thing you had to resolve before you traded your old life in for this one? And what about your wife? What did she think?

The interview goes on, but continues like this:

Do you ever take notes?

Not at first. But after a while, when they say something really good I ask, "May I write that down?" Then I take out the notebook and in the process of writing it down, I tell them why it is such a good quote, and exactly what it means to me and the book. My goal is for them to understand my project as well as I do. Because we're going to build the boat together. They are part t; they have a stake in it. Then I put the notebook away. And this drives them crazy. They'll spend the next six hours trying to make me *take my notebook out again!*

Conclusion

The important things to keep in mind with interviewing is to be prepared and don't be afraid to ask so-called "stupid" questions.

Interviewing can be one of the most exciting parts of the story-making process in creative non-fiction writing. You get to meet many interesting people – of course they would be interesting or you wouldn't be interviewing them. This is one of the many reasons people get into this type of work.

Also to keep in mind, keep a list of the sources you speak with and develop a database of your contacts. It is highly possible if you decide to stay in this career for the long-term, you will speak with your source again.

ASSIGNMENT

Choose someone to interview. They may be a police officer, a waitress, a local artist, a city councillour. Go through the steps in this chapter and prepare a Q & A, a question and answer report of the interview and post it to your personal website.

Here are some examples of open-ended questions:

1. How are you feeling today?
2. What makes you get up in the morning?
3. What are your plans for next year?
4. How do you make a living?
5. What's the most fun part of your day?
6. What's been the most special moment of your life so far?
7. What type of music do you like?

CHAPTER 8

USE OF SATIRE AND HUMOUR IN A STORY

Hello and welcome to chapter eight on the use of satire and humour in a story. I'll let you know right off the bat – I'm not that funny of a person until you get to know me a bit better. I'm much funnier in person. Writing humour is difficult, I encourage you to use your own instincts with this chapter and teach yourself as much as you can by absorbing media you find funny – especially creative non-fiction writing.

There's this guy that always passes by my house and hasn't ever said "hello" to me. He's younger than I am, but we are both alumni of where I did my undergraduate degree – Carleton University in Ottawa, Canada.

Is it the way I smell? – Yes, the days have been hot and it can be hard to smell "fresh." Is he judging me on my bad habits? – Whom the heck is he? Last time I checked Brad Pitt doesn't live in my neighbourhood – though I love the community where I live. Often I have days where I don't leave the area and I live in a big city.

Whatever the reason, there are so many things in life which can inspire humour. Like yesterday's rainfall when my Dad came to my door with a big box on his head. I didn't even recognize him at first.

Using satire and humour in your writing can be a great way to entertain your reader. Keeping things light-hearted – when it is called for can endear the reader to you, the writer. Here's a sample from *Utopia: Towards a New Toronto* edited by Jason McBride and Alana Wilcox. This selection is called "I love infrastructure" by Dale Duncan:

> I'm hiking through the woods of Algonquin Park with my nature-loving small-town friend Beth. Beth is one of those people who are always overflowing with curiosity, and here in Canada's largest provincial park, she's like a little kid at the Science Centre. Beth's interest in quirky details in one of her most

endearing qualities; she once took me gallivanting through an arboretum to net butterflies, stopping to categorize and record each specimen in her butterfly journal before setting it free.

Beth spent a summer working at Algonquin, and as we hike along a familiar trail, she tells me about Moth Boy, famous throughout the park for his love of everything to do with moths. The seventeen-year-old had snagged a good job working in the park as a naturalist that year due to his obsession with the natural environment; moths in particular were his passion. According to Beth, a one-hour walk with Moth Boy turned into two hours because, well, "he just loved to identify moths."

Nature often inspires such behaviour; there's always the cousin who stops to collect different rocks, the little boy who searches for snakes, or the aunt who points out various birds. It's hard, in fact, to find people who don't like nature, or, at least, those who admit to it. Everything's connected to nature. There's so much diversity, so much complexity. You can't hate nature. It's pure and innocent, tainted only by the hands of humans. To Beth, the city is cold and empty in comparison. It's representative of the follies of the human race: depressing, sterile and uninviting.

From the example above, Duncan uses satire and humour effectively by describing his friend Beth as "small-town." He calls the boy who loves moths – "Moth Boy" and also I've included the third paragraph where he reflects on nature with a more serious tone.

Duncan was able to switch from a light-hearted beginning to a serious tone by remaining consistent with his writing style. There is not a moment in the excerpt, or in the entire essay, where his "voice" doesn't seem to come through.

MID-CHAPTER ASSIGNMENT 8.1

"Moth Boy" – think of someone you can nickname for the purpose of a story.

"He's like a fat kid with a smarty" –. Comparisons are a common device used in humour. Think of a funny metaphor you can come up with that is unique.

"I'm so hungry I could eat a horse" – This is known as exaggeration. Many times exaggeration makes for great forms of comedy. Other examples of this include:

Q: Did he take the drivers exam?
A: He wrote the drivers exam

Try this kind of humour yourself

"He makes George Clooney looks like Alf" – this is a form of humour known as a people comparison and can often be used humorously because it is a ridiculous statement. When using this form of humour, you have to know who your audience is and make sure you're not insulting anyone. Give this form of humour a try.

This next selection comes from William Zinsser in *On Writing Well*. He comments on using humour in writing this way:

Humor is the secret weapon of the nonfiction writer. It's secret because so few writers realize that humor is often their best tool – and sometimes their only tool – for making an important point (Zinsser, 230).

He gives some examples of humourous incidents and writing:

> Luckily, my vigil was at last rewarded. I was browsing at a newsstand and saw four magazines side by side: Hairdo, Celebrity Hairdo, Combout and Pouf. I bought all four – to the alarm of the news dealer – and found a whole world of journalism devoted solely to hair: life from the neck up, but not including the brain. The magazines had diagrams of elaborate roller positions, and they also had columns in which a girl could send her roller problem to the editors for their advice. That was what I needed. I invented a magazine called Haircurl and wrote a series of parody letter s and replies. The piece ran in Life and it began like this:

Dear Haircurl:

I am 15 and am considered pretty in my group. I wear baby pink rollers, jumbo size. I have been going steady with a certain boy for 21/2 years and he has never seen me without my rollers. The other night I took them off and we had a terrible fight. "Your head looks small," he told me. He called me a dwarf and said I had misled him. How can I win him back?

HEARTSICK
Speonk, N.Y.

Dear Heartsick:

You have only yourself to blame for doing something so stupid. The latest "Hair-curl" survey shows that 94% of American girls now wear rollers in their hair 21.6 hours a day and 359 days a year. You tried to be different and you lost your fella. Take our advice and get some super-jumbo rollers (they come in your favorite baby pink shade, too) and your head will look bigger than ever and twice as lovely. Don't ever take them off again.

Comedians like Eddie Murphy, Chris Rock, Will Farrell, Ellen Degeneres and Whoopi Goldberg have made profitable careers from being funny. Part of the reason I'm sure why Whoopi Goldberg gave named herself as such is because it sounds funny.

Draw from what brings a smile to your face, makes you laugh, makes others laugh, etc. to add humour to your stories.

Remember satire is a form of humour which usually makes fun of life in some way. It's closely related to irony. Just as with any good comedy sketch, you need to have good pacing, timing and structure.

The best way to know how to do humour is through exposing yourself to as much funny stuff as you can. It is widely understood in writing circles that through exposure and constant and consistent reading – you will be able to better understand the concepts I'm teaching and writing here.

Conclusion

The use of satire and humour in stories is a powerful weapon because it can engage your readers – help you to connect more with your audience. If you don't find yourself a particularly funny person – get inspiration from books, movies, songs, comedians, even emails that make you laugh. Laughter does the soul good.

ASSIGNMENT

Write a one page story that includes humour and satire. To encourage peer review, plus the review from myself – post your assignment to your personal website. Humor is an extremely subjective thing. The only thing I ask as your instructor is that refuse to read and grade anything that is vulgar or is an insult to any cultural, religious, political, etc. group. Some of you may think these rules out all comedy. That should make this assignment all the more interesting because then it's more of a challenge.

CHAPTER 9

ORGANIZING YOUR TIME AND BUSINESS AS A WRITER

If one wants to write, one simply has to organize one's life in a mass of little habits.
- Graham Green (1904-1991)

Hello and welcome to chapter nine on organizing your time and business as a writer. Working in writing can take on many different forms. You may be working in an office where you are the junior to senior writer on in-house projects. You may be working in corporate communications with a bank. You may be a "beat" reporter, covering education for your local newspaper. You may be a freelance communicator, like I am, running your own business with clients you need to answer to and deliver "the goods."

I imagine the reason why many of you are taking this ebook is because you would like to get into any of the above scenarios – plus, the writing life offers a whole lot more.

Let's start with discussing working as an in-house writer. For every industry you can think of and every business, writers are needed. If you choose to work the 9-5 deal many people are in, you're day is already structured. You may need to work overtime and on weekends (even holidays) to get things done – but, this is part of any job.

What I'd like to concentrate on are the pluses and the minuses of working from home or on contract as a writer. I don't plan to be negative about this kind of work – I do it and I enjoy it. However, there are some things that will aid in your at-home office set-up.

If you plan on starting on your own writing or communications business, I suggest trying to get a copy of *The Wealthy Writer* by Michael Meanwell. The Writer's Digest *Handbook of Magazine Article Writing* edited by Michelle Ruberg is also a good source. I will supply you with necessary information here.

Are you ready for business?

Meanwell notes a list of questions to ask yourself before starting out with your own business. If you answer "no" to some of these questions, it may not mean that you are not ready to start your own business – it could be an indication of how successful you will be initially. However, circumstances have a way of changing and as some of the "no" answers turn into "yes" answers, you may start to see your profits soar.

- Are you willing to dedicate long hours for low wages?
- Are you healthy?
- Is your family supportive?
- Have you ever been self-employed?
- Have you worked as a full-time writer before?
- Are you disciplined with money?
- Are you disciplined with time?
- Are you self-motivated?
- Are you good with people?
- Are you a good leader?
- Are you responsible?
- Are you a good decision-maker?

These are some things to keep in mind with owning your own communications or writing business.

Business Plan

One of the first things you want to do before you start your own business is write a business plan. This is basically like your own manifesto for your business.

At the same time, you also need to discover a name for your business. I once read in the Freelancing for Dummies book that it was good to name your business in your own name. That's what I do. However, if you have a snazzy title for your business and get it registered or incorporated where you live – you're off to a good start. Some people do not officially register their business and do quite well. The choice is yours.

In your business plan you want to include the following information:

- What field will you service?
- Who is your competition?
- What advantages do you have over the competition? For example, the all important question to this aspect is why should a company hire you?
- Can you deliver a better product, service, or solution?
- What are your skills and experience, and how can they benefit the business?
- What is the best legal structure for the business?
- How should you keep your business records?
- What insurance do you need? This could be important because you may need to buy into a health insurance package that could protect you if for some reason you can't work
- How will you attract business?
- How will you operate? This includes how will you structure your day?
- Do you need a financial strategy?
- What equipment will you need?
- What will you name your business?
- What space do you need to run a business?

These are all things to keep in mind when you're starting your business. Here are some wise words from Meanwell:

Getting Organized

Quality practitioners get it right the first time, every time. The secret of their success relates to systems: a set of procedures developed to ensure that every aspect of their business is coordinated professional and efficiently.

Here are some tips from Meanwell on how to organize your files and information while writing and keeping your business running smoothly:

- Coding files for easy recall: this includes systems such as "PER" for personal files and "HSE" for house files
- Managing information on your desk and computer: suggestions include setting up a separate folder for each client – this is something I do as well

- Dealing with snail mail and email: Meanwell suggests getting that done at the end of the day. Since some of my business is online, I check more frequently
- Backing up data: make sure you keep all your important files on disks or discs to guard against not being to access them from your hard drive
- Handling office supplies and repairs: keep a list of suppliers and "fix-it" people at your fingertips

Six Easy Habits for Improving Efficiency from Meanwell:

1. Keep it clean
2. Plan each task each day
3. Keep a shopping list
4. Get into a routine
5. Do tasks in batches
6. When you're hot, don't stop

Meanwell also goes into some tips about working from home. There are some things I can suggest as well.

If you have a huge household to manage or share duties with others, consider renting office space. This can be an extremely efficient way to deal with your time and separate your home life from your work life.

There are many office buildings where you can use their fax machines, bring a laptop or they have computers, get all the services of a receptionist, etc. for low prices.

If you have the space and the comfort to work from home – try to section off a convenient place for work. In this case, the kitchen table won't do. It truly helps to have your own room just for work.

You can keep whatever policy you like for your office space – personnel only, or allow the occasional person to enter – whatever you like – you're the boss. You may find working styles you've experienced in the past will encourage you adopt those habits at home if they worked well for you.

There are times where you may want to keep your answering machine on during off hours. While you're working, you may want to make every effort to answer on the first one or two rings like I was taught in the provincial government of Ontario, Canada. Whatever your style, make sure it works for you and your clients.

The style of your writing life must suit your needs as well as your clients. In the book *The New New Journalism*, there are stories about writers whom get up first thing in the morning and write in the mornings, go take a break, then get back to it for the afternoon. There are other stories about people who only write at night. Julia Cameron's *The Right to Write* suggests writing in the mornings and calls this practice "morning pages."

I suggest whatever style suits you best is what you need to go with. Finding time to write, especially if you haven't quit your day job yet, can be difficult. There are many stories about people who will even sneak some time to write while they are working. While I was working as a Media Librarian, I would do this in the quiet time and often was inspired to do my work quickly and efficiently just so I could get time to write. I was able to publish the story I was working on.

Conclusion

Getting organized is the key to a successful writing career whether you work for yourself or for a company, non-profit, NGO (non-governmental organization), government or on community projects. If you work a 9 to 5 job, the structure is already set for you and you may find you still find to work extra hours to get the jobs done.

When you work for yourself, it's much of the same thing. You have to be willing to put in the hours wherever you can find them. Keeping your clients happy is the number one objective for yourself and them. Equally important, keeping yourself happy and healthy is the number objective for you, your family and your friends.

ASSIGNMENT

If you plan to own your own business – set up a business plan with the above guidelines, answering the questions and post your assignment to your personal website.

- What field will you service?
- Who is your competition?
- What advantages do you have over the competition? For example, the all important question to this aspect is why should a company hire you?
- Can you deliver a better product, service, or solution?
- What are your skills and experience, and how can they benefit the business?
- What is the best legal structure for the business?
- How should you keep your business records?
- What insurance do you need? This could be important because you may need to buy into a health insurance package that could protect you if for some reason you can't work
- How will you attract business?
- How will you operate? This includes how will you structure your day?
- Do you need a financial strategy?
- What equipment will you need?
- What will you name your business?
- What space do you need to run a business?

CHAPTER 10

WRITING FOR THE INTERNET

Hello and welcome to chapter 10 on writing for the Internet. It's been a pleasure chatting with all of you and reading your stuff online. Without the Internet, we would not all be together in this wonderful way that I have intended.

The most important thing to keep in mind when writing for the Internet is to write in the inverted pyramid method mentioned in chapter two.

Many websites also greatly condense information because people are more likely to shift their attention on the 'net by surfing through information. The way many websites solve this problem is by providing 400 to 500 words of text that will give you the gist of a story on any size screen.

Here's some advice on how to write for the Internet from Darlene Maciuba-Koppel from *The Web Writer's Guide: Tips and Tools*:

>Online writing requires a new way of thinking for print authors. As you begin your first draft, start training yourself to write in short chunks of information. (You can storyboard your draft on index cards or use your word processing software to create an outline.) Begin to develop subheadings and topic sentences for each information chunk. This step will help you organize your information and create a natural flow throughout your document.

>During your writing, think about internal links that you might add within your site that offer readers more detailed information. Decide on external links to other sites that can enhance your document's value (e.g. a link to a reputable reference site listed at the end of your article).

>While writing your first draft, remember that your text should be easy to scan. Reading text on screens is more difficult than reading print copy. Make it

easy for your online readers by writing meaningful headings and subheadings so they will be prepared for the copy that follows. Creatively written headings and subheadings can also grab readers' attention and cause them to keep reading copy they might otherwise pass over. Tight writing is even more important on the Web. Shorter sentences and simple words make your copy reader-friendly. Strip your copy of unnecessary words and phrases (Maciuba-Koppel, 9).

Maciuba-Koppel also gives pointers on the importance of editing your online copy:

After you have written your first draft, it's time to let your copy cool down. Only then should you begin to edit your document. You'll come back to your copy with a fresh perspective and more easily spot errors and clumsy prose. To make sure you produce a high-quality and error-free document, you should follow a specific set of procedures during the editing process. If you are responsible for all the content on a site, you do this by developing an in-house style guide and a customized Editorial Checklist that meets the needs of your particular Web site. If you have a complex Web site, you may have to develop an Editorial Checklist for each category of your Web site.

Another avenue where you may want to try your hand at writing online is with newsletters. Here are some words from Maciuba Koppel:

E-mail newsletters offer many advantages. A well-written newsletter gives you the opportunity to instantly communicate with your subscribers through the personal medium of e-mail. Printing and distribution costs are no longer a concern. Once subscribers learn that they can depend on you for useful information, they come to see you as a valuable resource. By appearing in your subscribers' inbox on a consistent basis, you get the change to remind readers about your site and encourage them to make return visits.

John Funk, creator of InfoBeat, suggests that one of the most important things to focus on if you want to succeed with e-mail publications is the end-user experience. He says that an e-mail publication is not about you; it's about the end user. Every interaction your reader has that relates to your e-mail newsletter should be a positive experience.

Conclusion

Writing for the eye and the ear can lead to many interesting careers in advertising, television, radio, marketing, the gaming industry, as well as the Internet.

ASSIGNMENT

Your assignment is to create a blog using www.blogsource.com or www.myspace.com. It's a great free site based in California which I use on my website: www.donnakakonge.com. All the instructions you need to create one are on the site and just follow the instructions. When you've done your first posting, invite everyone on your personal website to visit your blog and I'll take a peek.

CHAPTER 11

TOOLS OF SELF-EDITING

Hello and welcome to chapter eleven on the tools of self-editing. The editor is an important part of the writing process. There are many jobs that can be found in editing and every writer needs a good editor. An important thing to keep in mind is every writer needs to know how to edit their material. There are some tricks to make it helpful and effective:

- Read your copy out loud – if you stumble on a word, it probably needs to be reworded
- Use dictionaries, thesauri, and books like Strunk and White's The Elements of Style for grammar use and vocabulary expansion
- Books like On Writing Well by William Zinsser can also give you great advice on how to write and is a well-respected source of material in the field
- Always use the spell-check functions on your word processing software before you hand in a creative non-fiction assignment to an editor

There are other things to keep in mind as well:

- Always look for where you can edit words like "that" and "which"
- Try to write in complete sentences, with the exception of visual media – sometimes phrases can come in handy

Here are some final words from Zinsser's *On Writing Well*:

> Clutter is the disease of American writing. We are a society strangling in unnecessary words, circular constructions, pompous frills and meaningless jargon.
>
> Who can understand the viscous language of everyday American commerce: the memo, the corporation report, the business letter, the notice from

the bank explaining its latest, "simplified" statement? What member of a insurance or medical plan can decipher the brochure explaining his costs and benefits? What father or mother can put together a child's toy from the instructions on the box? Our national tendency is to inflate and thereby sound important. The airline pilot who announces that he is presently anticipating experiencing considerable precipitation wouldn't think of saying it may rain. The sentence is too simple – there must be something wrong with it.

But the secret of good writing is to strip every sentence to its cleanest components. Every word that serves no function, every long world that could be a short word, every adverb that carries the same meaning that's already in the verb, every passive construction that leaves the reader unsure of who is doing what – these are the thousand and one adulterants that weaken the strength of a sentence. And they usually occur in proportion to education and rank (Zinsser, 2006).

This is an important thing to note as your writing your copy and also self-editing for it to receive final review from your editor.

Conclusion

Self-editing is an important tool in knowing how to simplify language and keep copy clean. Before you give your final assignment to an editor, it's important to deliver a product as free from error as possible.

ASSIGNMENT

Read the article below and make it more precise by cutting out less important elements and rewording the article as necessary. This assignment is meant to teach you how to how to be brief with your writing without loosing the essence of the message your trying to convey. Once you have rewritten the article to be shorter, upload your work to your personal website for review.

Here is an excerpt from a short story collection called *The New Story Writers* edited by John Metcalf. This selection is from Douglas Glover called "The Obituary Writer":

We drifted along in this empire of death like accursed phantoms
-de Ségur

Aiden is in St.Joseph's, dying of head injuries. Annie has gone Catholic on me. She has quite school and taken a job at a home for retarded children in West Saint John. She works the graveyard shift so she can spend the day with Aiden. Mornings, she visits the hospital chapel for mass. I hardly ever see her.

Of all the brothers and sisters (there are a dozen O'Reillys, counting the parents), Aiden and Annie were closest in age and sympathy, though all they ever did in public was bicker and complain about one another. Aiden was the family clown, a bespectacled, jug-eared, loud-mouthed ranter, given to taunting the younger children and starting fights – though he once sang in the cathedral choir and spent a year trying to teach himself the guitar. Annie is boyish and prim. She dawdles over her make-up, ties her red hair back and gets average grades in her university ebooks. But like many people who spend their lives reining themselves in, she has a soft spot in her heart for eccentrics and outsiders. One always knew that if anything happened to Aiden, it would be hardest on Annie. It is also natural that she should flail about, trying to locate beyond herself an agent responsible for this terrible tragedy. I say "beyond herself" on purpose, because, of course, Annie O'Reilly blames herself for everything first. Then me.

Mornings, in the chapel, she and God are sorting all this out. But I have little hope that He will see fit to represent my side of things.

CHAPTER 12

GETTING PUBLISHED

Hello and welcome to one of the most important chapters – getting published, chapter 12. This is the important part. Like I said before, your brilliant work will do no one any good by sitting in a shoe box under your bed. You have to help your work see the light, even if you write at night. There are many ways to do this.

I've already mentioned many books and articles like Michael Meanwell's *The Wealthy Writer* which has great suggestions on getting published. As many of you may be starting out, some of things you may want to try are some tips I'll mention here. We'll get back to Meanwell's book later:

• Scour your neighbourhood for free publications that may pay writers to deliver content
• Go on the web and check out e-zines and websites that may need content
• Develop your own website and publish your material there – any time you publish something to the web that is an act of publishing. So if you completed the blog assignment you are already published?
• Check out your local newspapers and community newspapers to find out if you can write for them
• Buy writers guides and writers magazines with a list of places where you can publish

These are just some suggestions. You also need to know the market for your story ideas before you start writing. By using writer's markets guides, you can discover which publications would be interested in your work. Keeping track of this in a file or a report will make your work to find work easier.

Once you've found the markets to pitch your ideas, you need to write a query letter.

Query Letters

Query letters are an important part of your dialogue with an editor to get your work published. It is a basically a letter to an editor containing these essential elements:

- What your story idea is and how it would benefit the magazine or newspaper's market
  - Who you are? What experience you bring to the magazine or newspaper?
  - Contact information on how to get a hold of you
- A note that you will be following up on the query letter after a period of four to six weeks for a magazine and about a week for a newspaper (depending on how timely the story is)

You need to use your best writing when doing a query. This also becomes an example of your work. You may also want to point the editor in the direction of where they can find samples of work through your website, or attach samples of your work with the email.

The editor needs to know not only do you have a great idea that will help them to sell magazines, newspapers or increase the number of hits on their site, they need to know you will do the work well. This goes back to chapter 11, they need to know they won't be wasting time re-writing and correcting your work.

Journalism and writing is a competitive market and you always need to fine-tune the craft. Publishing is a chapter in experience and it's important to do this as often as you can.

Here's sample query letter from *Guide to Writing Magazine Non-fiction* by Michael Bugeja:

0000 Main Street
Athens, Ohio 00000

April 17, 1997

Jean P. Kelly, Editor
Ohio Magazine
62 E. Broad Street
Columbus, Ohio 43215-3522

Dear Jean Kelly:

One of the most successful environmental efforts in the last 25 years has been the miraculous restoration of Lake Erie. In 1972 some scientist believed that the effects of massive pollution and intensive commercial shoreline development upon the lake were irreversible.

Scientists in a Toledo-based research group are optimistic that people are learning to make reasonable tradeoffs between their need to develop the lake shoreline and maintain the lake's ecological integrity. An unlikely combination of luck, governmental support, public awareness and scientific ingenuity ahs rescued the lake.

I would like to send you a 2,000-word article, "The Miracle of Lake Erie," for your "Environment" department. As this is the 25th anniversary of the lake's cleanup, I plan to show how far the lake has come and its prognosis for the next 10 to 15 years.

I am a write with more than 10 years' experience in public relations and journalism. I am working toward a master's degree in journalism at Ohio University.

I look forward to hearing from you and have enclosed a stamped, self-addressed envelope for your reply.

Sincerely,

Les Roka
(555) 555-5555

MID-CHAPTER ASSIGNMENT 12.1

Using the example above, write a query letter about a story idea you have for one of the magazines you have at home. Make sure it follows the same format.

You can also choose to write an e-mail query letter that would be similar in format, but sent through electronic mail. You can post that one to your personal website for review and then send it off to a magazine for real. Usually the waiting time to find out if an editor wants your story with e-mail is much shorter than with snail mail.

Ebooks

Another increasinging your cache as a writer is to publish an ebook. Michael Meanwell's book *The Wealthy Writer* first started as an ebook called *The Enterprising Writer*. It later turned into a traditional book.

Here are some words from Meanwell on how to become an E-Publisher:

> There are a couple of reasons why you should establish your own Web site.
>
> First, you retain the maximum percentage of profits. Once you've set up your site, you will only need to pay for your ongoing Web hosting and domain fees as well as charges for accepting payments via credit cards. Depending on which providers you select, these costs may represent 5 to 10 percent of the cost of each sale.
>
> Second, by establishing your own site, you have the opportunity to not only promote and sell your books but also showcase your other literary works and skills, and attract more business.
>
> While the rewards can be high, you will need to make a serious investment in understanding how Web marketing works and how to attract and convert visitors to customers – all before you see a serious financial return. If you decide to build your own site, there are many online tools that can help you as well as some good, low-cost, easy-to-use Web development packages.

As stated earlier, the key to Web site success, particularly in our profession, is to keep it simple. The added advantage in doing this is that you do not need to buy expensive Web development programs or hire a Web designer. Your priority should be to design simple Web pages, build credibility with quality products, stimulate interest with convincing copy, and have the ability to safely accept credit card payments and allow ebook downloads from your site. There's a significant investment to be made before you have a successful e-publishing venture, but I assure you that the long-term rewards far outweigh the initial investment.

What you also find here is an analysis or a review as discussed in chapter two, but this important information for getting your information and creative non-fiction published. Hopefully you will find with these guidelines, this ebook will turn out to be a wonderful investment for you.

Once you've completed an ebook you can use www.lulu.com to sell it. They are a great site that take only a small commission of sales, allow downloadable products and from a technology and security standpoint work great with ebooks. It's also pretty easy to set up for people without much ecommerce experience.

Dealing with Rejection

There is a lot of potential rejection to face with writing. Not everyone will say "yes" to your ideas and concepts. Not everyone may think you're good writer – especially in the beginning when you're first starting out. You need to believe in yourself and your talents and understand that you can't please everyone all the time.

Try to turn rejection into a victory by getting back up on the horse, so to speak, and just keep trying. Use rejection as fuel to try harder.

If you're running your own writing and years pass by without making any money – perhaps it may be time for you to shift gears. Try to think of the styles of writing that people have complimented you on. Is it your sales copy? Is it your hard-news stories? Is it your fiction work?

Although this ebook is a creative non-fiction one, there are many elements here which can translate into different forms of writing. Good writing is good writing. If you find this is your passion and you work hard – you will do well.

Here are some websites to get you started on your way to getting published:

www.getafreelancer.com: this website gives you the chance to register and bid for projects so you can get published with everything from copywriting to ebooks.

www.freelanceworkexchange.com: this another site where you need to register and bid for projects.

canadacareerarts@gmail.com: if you live in Canada, you may want to check out Don Joyce's Toronto Tonight Magazine

jobs@swaggnews.com: you may be interested in hip hop music and this magazine is looking for writers

www.craigslist.org: this is a great website for looking for writing and even television, radio and film projects in your area

www.associatedcontent.com: this website is powered by Google and allows you to become a content producer building your own website with articles – it's even possible you can make money if you generate enough traffic to your site.

www.suite101.com: this website which is based in Canada but has German business partners and is geared to a worldwide audience. You may be able to write about a specific topic like world affairs and build your own site.

www.concordia.ca: I'm alumni of Concordia University, and there is opportunity to write for the magazines of the schools you are alumni.

www.myspace.com: this is a place where you can look for jobs and create your own space on the Internet in a community of friends.

www.youtube.com: just bought out by Google, YouTube is huge and you can turn the scripts you've handed into me for class into reality by posting on this site.

www.blogsource.com: this free site based in California allows you to run your own blog and to publish as often as your time allows.

www.facebook.com: connects with a community of people to potentially share your writing.

Conclusion

Getting published is an important part of the game of establishing yourself as a writer. Many suggestions have been made here by contacting your local newspapers, checking out free magazines, publishing stuff on the Internet and creating your own site with ebooks.

Best of luck with publishing!

ASSIGNMENT

- Your assignment is to get your first piece published either in a newspaper, in a magazine online or offline. Whether or not you receive payment is not important at the beginning – just get published – this will help you do well in this ebook.

CHAPTER 13

FINAL WORDS ON WRITING AND FINAL ASSIGNMENT

Hello again for the last time and farewell to this ebook – it's been a pleasure. There are some people that say writing is the hardest job to do – I think it's the most wonderful job to do, including teaching it.

Yes, it's a tough profession. There are about a half a million writers in the United States alone, about five per cent of them get published. However, with the Internet, all of that is changing. The best advice I can give to you is to start your own website. Plus network with other writers and anyone you can meet so you can develop contacts and story ideas. The aim is to have a balanced life outside the solitude which can come with writing.

I hope you have found these chapters created by myself, Donna Kakonge, to be useful in your quest to make writing a substantial part of your life. Whether you do it part-time, full-time or occasionally, you will find it will become an important part of your life. To become a true professional, you must continue practicing for your entire life.

Good luck on your journey!

At this point you need to complete your final assignment. As well, don't forget to update your resume to include the completion of this ebook. With that, here is the final assignment.

FINAL ASSIGNMENT

Going back to chapter one and using all of the techniques you have learned in this ebook, write a creative non-fiction piece of no more than 10 pages and post to your personal website .

If you choose to write a memoir: write the first chapter of your memoir, no longer than 10 pages of a word processing program. Make sure it's single spaced and formatted similar to how you've seen these chapter plans.

If you choose to write a personal essay: the personal essay should be no longer than four pages and follow the guidelines in chapter one.

If you choose to write a feature: the feature should be about two to three pages in length and follow the guidelines in chapter one.

If you choose to write a profile: the profile should be no longer than three pages and include other sources than your protagonist or main subject for the piece.

If you choose to write a travel piece: the piece should be about three pages and describe a place in-depth following the guidelines in chapter one.

If you choose to write an analysis and a review: the review should be about a movie, a book, a play, a television show, etc. and be no longer than three pages.

Good luck with that as well! It's been a pleasure presenting this ebook to you.